AS Levels

Dedicated to
Bobby and Clem

AS Levels:
Implications for Schools,
Examining Boards and
Universities

Edited by
James J. Hughes
Pro Vice-Chancellor
University of Kent at Canterbury

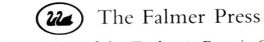 The Falmer Press

(A member of the Taylor & Francis Group)
London • New York • Philadelphia

UK   The Falmer Press, Falmer House, Barcombe, Lewes, East Sussex, BN8 5DL

USA   The Falmer Press, Taylor & Francis Inc., 242 Cherry Street, Philadelphia, PA 19106-1906

First published 1989

British Library Cataloguing in Publication Data

AS Levels: implications for schools, examining boards and universities.
  1. England. Secondary schools. GCE (AS level) courses.
  I. Hughes, James J. (James Joseph)
  373.19
  ISBN 1-85000-596-6
  ISBN 1-85000-597-4 (pbk.)

Jacket design by Caroline Archer

Typeset by Graphicraft Typesetters Ltd, Hong Kong

Printed in Great Britain by Taylor & Francis (Printers) Ltd, Basingstoke

Contents

Contents

Acknowledgements

Dreaming up ideas for a conference, even pencilling in the names of potential speakers, is a relatively easy task. It is when the conference theme has been decided and the speakers have agreed to participate that the real work of organization begins. In the case of this conference Mary Hedges assumed the organizer role, almost single-handed. No matter has been too big or too small for her. She has done a hundred and one things, all with great efficiency and the smooth running of the conference is entirely attributable to her efforts. In addition Mary Hedges has also played an important part in preparing this manuscript for publication. First, she organized a small team of typists to help her type up the tapes of all the conference sessions. Second, she undertook most of the typing and retyping of subsequent drafts. My indebtedness to her is considerable. Those who helped her in one or other of the typing stages are Wendy Lawson, Ros Webb, Jane Dring and Jo Maynard. To each I offer my thanks.

Preface

This book is based upon the proceedings of a conference held at the University of Kent at Canterbury at the end of June 1988. My colleague, Ron Flaherty, is the one who first proposed that we hold a conference on the important subject of Advanced Supplementary (AS) levels, the idea occurring to him as he listened to Professor Clive Wake address a group of sixth form advisers on the subject. That was in the summer of 1987, some two months before the first AS courses began. During the twelve months between the germination of the idea and the conference itself quite a lot happened. The first cohort of students taking AS courses almost completed the first year of those courses. The Higginson Report, *Advancing A levels*, was published and its main recommendation, for five leaner fitter courses, was rejected by government — although we had to wait for the conference itself for a fuller statement, by Robert Jackson, of the reasons behind the government's rejection. By the time the book is published the first AS level examinations will be upon us and shortly after that the first cohort of students with AS qualifications will be entering courses in higher education.

When we decided to go ahead with the conference we sought external advice on the programme and on speakers, and one of those to whom we turned for this advice was Clive Wake. Of course, he is no stranger to Kent, but his past links with the University were not the reason why, on this occasion, we turned to him. The reason was that he, perhaps more than anyone else, has been at the centre of discussions on, and developments in, AS levels since their inception, for most of which time he has been Secretary of SCUE. In addition to providing the inspiration for the conference and advice on its planning, Clive Wake was also one of the speakers in the first session of the conference and acted as chairman of the second. Clearly, our debt to him is enormous and he deserves a major share of the credit for the success of the conference. Furthermore, although they will never know it, those entering the sixth form over the next few years will be indebted to Clive Wake for the role that he has played in getting AS levels accepted more quickly than might otherwise have been the case.

Finally, it is perhaps worth mentioning that if we were planning the conference now we would, I think, with the benefit of hindsight, have invited more university admissions people to it. The reason is quite simply that — as became clear during the first session of the conference — those responsible for advising sixth formers about the choices open to them in higher education are deeply suspicious of the universities' admissions process, particularly the way in which it will treat applicants with AS levels rather than traditional A levels. A realization of how deep these suspicions are is certainly necessary before the universities consciously set about tackling them. There is a need to establish greater trust between the universities and the schools and if more university people had been at the conference this would have helped in the process of creating a climate of trust. Since universities other than Kent were not well represented at the conference this process may take a little longer. As a second best, I hope that those responsible for admitting students to university courses will read what follows.

James J. Hughes
December, 1988

Section I
The Universities and Broadening

Welcome and Opening Remarks

D.J.E. Ingram

Good morning, ladies and gentlemen, and a very warm welcome to the University of Kent at Canterbury. Could I also welcome you to this particular conference which is going to discuss AS levels and their implications for the schools, the examining boards and the universities. We have been very encouraged by the amount of interest shown in this conference. There are just on 300 schools and local authorities represented here today, and I am pleased to report that those attending are not just from the southern counties — although there are certainly a lot from the south — but many of them are from the north, with quite a few from places such as Liverpool and Manchester. I am also very glad to see that we have several of the international schools represented here. I am sure that topics such as the International Baccalaureate are going to enter into our discussions, so it is very important that the international schools are represented. We also have, as you know, representatives from the Secondary Examinations Council; the Schools Curriculum Development Committee; the examining boards — which occupy a crucial position between the schools and the universities — and the universities themselves. The latter are represented by Professor Clive Wake from the central office of the Standing Conference on University Admissions, as well as several colleagues from the University of Kent. There should therefore be a real mixing of viewpoints and experiences at this conference.

There is no doubt whatsoever that the topic of AS levels is of intense interest at the moment to all of us; schools, examining boards and universities. I know there has been quite a lot of argument about them and that there are still some who disapprove of them, but the fact is that they are here and already being taught. I realize that tomorrow especially, when we have the Minister with us, there may be questions about the Higginson Report and other alternatives. However, at the beginning of the conference it seems right to concentrate on the fact that AS levels are now in existence and explore the ways in which we can make the most of them. Maybe I could just set the scene by reminding you that, certainly from the universities' point of view, AS levels are up and running and are being discussed in great detail. In *University Entrance: The Official Guide* — the latest version of which is just out — you will see that we have made it·quite clear how seriously universities are taking AS levels. It shows that as far as the general requirement is concerned *all* universities will accept the following combinations as satisfying the five subject entry requirement. Two A levels plus two AS levels plus one O level or GCSE *or* two A levels plus one AS level plus two O levels or GCSEs. In other words, as far as meeting the general entry requirement is concerned, there is already considerable scope for AS levels within the sixth form curriculum.

In addition to meeting the general requirement students do, of course, have to meet course requirements. In order to see whether AS levels meet course requirements you will have to study in more detail *University Entrance*. You will find that in the subject pages we have put open symbols to indicate the subjects where AS levels are accepted instead of the normal A level requirements. For instance, if one were to take chemistry as a typical case, you will find that there are no less than twelve universities that will accept AS level chemistry instead of A level chemistry as an entrance requirement. Universities are making the situation absolutely clear in *University Entrance* that they regard AS levels as a real way of broadening the sixth form syllabus. These details are going to be dealt with in the conference, and I am sure that Professor Wake will be explaining how *University Entrance* itself should be used, and all the implications behind it. My job is not to do that, but to set the scene and to welcome you to the University.

In this connection I should make it clear that we in the University of Kent are very conscious of the need for broadening; we have, in a sense, tried to achieve this ever since we were created, just on twenty-five years ago. We have tried in two ways; one is through the collegiate system, with which you have already had some contact. You will have seen that our students not only live in the colleges at the University of Kent, but that a great deal of the teaching — most of the non-science teaching, in fact — takes place in the colleges, which include lecture theatres and seminar rooms as well as offices for academic staff. As a result, students are bound to bump into each other; they meet and have coffee or lunch with students studying other subjects as well as academics, and this we reckon is one of the best ways of broadening at the university level, mixing people so that ideas are bound to bounce off one another. In short, the collegiate system is a means of integrating teaching and residence and provides one of the major ways we attempt to introduce broadening into our curriculum.

The other way in which we have attempted to achieve some broadening· has been through our courses. As is the case at many universities, in part I of our degrees we have a broad approach entailing several subjects before students go on to specialize at part II. But in addition we also offer students the opportunity of taking interdisciplinary courses, particularly in our humanities and social sciences faculties. Therefore, the spirit of AS levels already exists at the University of Kent. We do believe in a broader approach to teaching and learning and we believe that the introduction of AS levels into sixth form studies will widen the horizon of those coming into the universities.

Now, enough from me. Let me just explain how we intend to organize this first session, where we have two main speakers. The first talk by Dr. Kingdon sets the scene by describing the earlier attempts to broaden the curriculum and explaining why these failed. In the second Professor Wake discusses the universities' response to the AS proposal. Since these talks are clearly related to each other I would propose that we take the first talk by Dr. Kingdon and then go straight on to the talk by Professor Wake. This will ensure plenty of time for discussion of both the papers at the end of the talks. Also, given that a number of questions and comments may well overlap this seems the most sensible way of proceeding.

Dr. Kingdon, who is a former science teacher, is currently Head of Research at the University of London School Examinations Board and is well acquainted with both the school and university interests, problems and aspirations. He is therefore particularly well qualified to set the scene for us.

Professor Wake, who was previously a member of this university, is currently running what is called SCUE, the Standing Conference on University Entrance. This is concerned with the universities' overall view of the interface between schools and universities. It is often confused with UCCA, but UCCA is a purely technical organization that makes no decisions, it only makes sure that everything runs smoothly so far as university entrance is concerned.

It is SCUE that deals with all the difficult questions of principle and problems arising from the academic side of university admissions. So Clive Wake has really been right at the cutting edge as far as the question of university admission is concerned. He has not only been involved in the formulation of policy with respect to AS levels but for other qualifications too, such as that of Business and Technician Education Council (BTEC) and the International Baccalaureate, both of which have become increasingly important over recent years. He will be able to give us a very up-to-date view, and I am sure that he will confirm that we on the higher education side regard AS levels as not only a challenge but as a great opportunity too.

Reference

ASSOCIATION OF COMMONWEALTH UNIVERSITIES (1988) *University Entrance; The Official Guide, 1988*, London, ACU.

Chapter 1

Setting the Scene

M. Kingdon

Introduction

The traditional responsibilities of examination board researchers have been to conduct technical research into new and existing school examinations. Prompted by the introduction of the GCSE, the role has been extended to include research into the impact of new examinations upon students, teachers, and schools/colleges as a whole — work now extended to AS levels. Very occasionally examination board researchers are asked to consider the origins and development of existing ideas and procedures. In short, to attempt to answer questions of this form 'How do we come to be where we are now?' Both in this talk and the one this afternoon I shall endeavour to do all three, but in reverse order.

In 1988, thirty-seven years after the GCE Advanced level examinations were introduced, it is difficult to imagine the extent to which the early A levels were criticized for both their narrowness — and for the detrimental effects that this might have upon the setting of the curriculum — and, for their potential unreliability. Numerous attempts have been made since 1951 to broaden the setting for the curriculum by the introduction of structural — one might almost say revolutionary — reforms but, with the exception of the AS level proposals, these have been unsuccessful. The criticisms of technical inefficiency were resolved by the gradual, evolutionary, improvement of both syllabuses and examinations. This second process was successful and even by the early 1960s A levels had come to be seen as the embodiment of academic standards at 18+. A reluctance to tamper with A level standards seems to have been one of the main reasons for the repeated failure of the attempts at structural reform.

Three other movements have influenced the development of the sixth form curriculum and each of them is interwoven with the process of evolutionary development identified above. The first is the attempt to broaden and enrich the sixth form curriculum by the development of liberal and general studies courses. The former courses are usually not examined, while the latter are via GCE A, AO and, latterly, AS level syllabuses. The second movement is the development of 17+ — Alternative Ordinary Level (AO) and Certificate of Extended Education (CEE) — courses. The last of these movements has been the attempt to increase the accountability of the A level system. This movement has been exemplified by a desire to standardize syllabus content and to specify outcomes of A level courses. A parallel movement has been taking place within 16+ examinations.

This paper is primarily concerned with setting a context for the one successful attempt at structural change — the Advanced Supplementary level. Nevertheless, these other movements have played a major part, and still continue to play a part, in the development of AS levels.

1988 is not only the first year of the new GCSE examinations and the last year of AO levels, it is also the 150th anniversary of the first Matriculation examination of the University of London. (I make no apology for concentrating for a moment on the early examinations of my own University. The nineteenth-century initiatives that led to the GCSE and A level are very largely a history of the pre-degree examinations of the University of London.). The University of London Matriculation examinations were open to anybody over the age of 16. This examination was the forerunner of our present 16+ examinations and the GCSE. The curriculum for the Matriculation examination was not a narrow one: it had, for its day, a very wide span of subjects. In addition to the diet of classics and some mathematics that was being served up in many schools at the time, papers in natural philosophy (chemistry or botany) and English (language, history and geography) were included. The examination served as a University Entrance examination, as a means for the award of University scholarships and as a general educational qualification. As time passed further subjects were added and by the middle of the century a system of subject groups was established that some present today may recognize from their School Certificate Examinations. In short, the candidates who took the London examination and the other Matriculation examinations that appeared had, what even today we would call, a broad education.

The true origins of A levels, and perhaps the root of the problem that we are considering, lie in the expansion of degree courses that took place at the beginning of the second half of the nineteenth century. In 1859 London introduced two-part degrees. The first parts — which became known as the Intermediate examinations — could be taken one year after the Matriculation examination and like that examination were open to school candidates.

The Intermediate examinations were faculty examinations and the number and choice of subjects offered was therefore restricted. This pattern was carried over into the Higher School Certificate when it was started in the early years of the twentieth century. Indeed, as far as London was concerned, for many years the Intermediate candidates in the University and the Higher School Certificate candidates in the schools took the same papers.

Until just after World War I students could proceed from school to university degree via *either* the School Certificate, the Higher School Certificate and university entrance, *or* by Matriculation, university entrance and the Intermediate Examination. It was the pressure of a demobilizing soldiery that caused school pupils to defer university entrance and resulted in the Higher School Certificate becoming the dominant route.

The Higher School Certificate was not as narrow as A levels were to become. There was a system of main and subsidiary subjects and the basic university entrance requirements were either three main subject passes or two main subject passes plus two subsidiary passes. It is also worth remembering that many students did not in fact take subsidiary subjects, they merely gained 'subsidiary passes' on main subject examinations — something that certainly would not be allowed in the A and AS level system that we are to consider today.

Attempts at Structural Change in A Level Curriculum

There have been at least three major initiatives to reform A levels and the recent Higginson proposals constitute a fourth. These sets of proposals are of interest, not only because they anticipate several of the features of AS levels — this is especially true of the first set of proposals — but also because they are reflected to some extent in the strategies being used to teach AS levels.

The Major/Minor/General system (1960)

This was to have been a system of full and half A levels and had many similarities with the AS level proposals now being adopted. It was anticipated that two major and two minor subjects would be the standard pattern and even the ideas of contrasting and complementary combinations of subjects were proposed. In acknowledgement of developments within the sixth form population, it would also have been possible for students to pick a course of study consisting entirely of minor subjects — and this will of course be possible under the AS system.

The major/minor proposal coincided with a period of acute teacher shortage and it was believed that it would, if adopted, exacerbate the situation. In addition, the major universities were openly hostile to the major/minor idea — and therefore broadening of the curriculum was not achieved through this proposal. We should note in passing that this failure of the major/minor proposal may have led directly to the development of the International Baccalaureat.

A variation of the major/minor system was proposed in 1964 whereby major examinations were to be assessed externally and the minor subjects (electives) were to be conducted on a mode 3 basis. The idea, like its predecessor, did not find favour with the universities.

Qualifying and Further examinations (1967)

This proposal was produced in 1967 by the newly founded Schools Council. Students were to take a 17+ examination (the Qualifying level) in about five subjects and these would be used, instead of O levels, for initial application to higher education. Candidates would then take three of their five subjects to the Further level at 18+. The Q and F proposal was not adopted because of a number of fears: that three consecutive years of public examinations would have a detrimental effect upon the students; that there were insufficient teachers to operate it; and, that it would necessitate the extension of most university courses to four years.

Normal and Further levels (1973)

This proposal was the School Council's response to the failure of their Q and F ideas. Under this proposal students would typically have taken five subjects at 18+, of which two might be at Normal (N) level and three at Further (F) level. N levels were to require half the teaching and study time of F levels. As students would be studying the equivalent of four or more full courses, F level standards were not to be equated with those of A levels.

The N and F proposal failed to gain general acceptance despite the fact that it was very thoroughly researched. This was probably because its implementation would again have meant interfering with the A level system and the standards embodied in it.

Some observations

There are some lessons that could have been learnt from these earlier attempts at broadening the sixth form curriculum. Firstly, they tended to be more fully researched and discussed than the AS level proposal has been. Secondly, and partly as a result of this research and discussion, there was an inherent tendency to elaborate the basic idea often to the point where the schemes as a whole might have become unworkable. Lastly, and particularly in the case of the later proposals, interference with A levels had become almost sacrilegious. It is therefore worth stressing that AS levels do not seek to replace A levels but, as their name implies, supplement their provision.

I Levels

The failure of the repeated attempt to reform the structure of A levels also caused problems for 17+ students in schools and colleges. Two further examinations, the Alternative Ordinary level (AO) and Certificate of Extended Education (CEE) were developed in the mid 1970s. These were reviewed by the Keohane Committee (1979) whose recommendations were in turn considered by the government in a consultative paper, *Examinations 16–18*, published a year later. The latter document advanced the case for the introduction of 'a freestanding intermediate examination to be taken alongside A levels, normally at 18+'. Four years later the idea reappeared as the AS level proposal. It is paradoxical that the one successful attempt to reform the structure of GCE 18+ examinations has its origin in a 17+ examination.

AS Levels

When the AS level proposals are fully implemented students will have the opportunity to replace one or more of their A level courses by a larger number of AS level ones. In this way it is hoped that students will be able to continue more of their GCSE subjects — or indeed start some new ones — in the sixth. *This broadening is to be achieved without making extra demands upon the student and without any loss of academic rigour.*

Students will be able to broaden their sixth form courses by taking AS level subjects from both within and/or outside their specialist A level areas. These will be termed respectively *complementary* and *contrasting* combinations of subjects. An example of the first might be an A level scientist taking design and technology, and a humanities student continuing with mathematics would be an example of the second. The government has expressed the hope that all the students will take at least one contrasting subject. Some syllabuses have been designed as complementary or contrasting ones but, generally, AS level syllabuses are intended to be used in both sorts of combinations.

AS level syllabuses have been designed to take the study of a subject to the *same depth* as corresponding A levels, but to make *half of the demands in terms of teaching and study time.* (Or rather, it is intended that two AS levels should make the same intellectual and time demands as one A level.) The issue of how these aims are to be achieved will be considered in greater detail in my second presentation this afternoon.

AS levels are intended as examinations for the ablest 18-year-olds who have taken two year courses and who are also taking A levels. There is, of course, nothing to prevent schools or students attempting AS level examinations at 17+ and/or after one year of study. Similarly, there are no requirements as to the number of AS levels or A levels that any student must study. As the foregoing summaries have indicated, none of these features of the AS level examination, including the idea of complementary and contrasting combinations of subjects, are entirely new to 18+ examinations.

In one sense the AS level proposal might be judged as the most successful of the attempts to broaden the sixth form curriculum — certainly it is the only proposal to have been implemented. One of the main advantages that it has is its flexibility; it is possible within the A/AS system to produce a wide variety of sixth form courses and so serve the needs of different groups of candidates. Further, AS levels are likely to succeed because all relevant bodies — higher education, schools and colleges, employers and especially the Department of Education and Science — have pledged their support; support that most of these bodies denied to the previous proposals for structural reform.

The Evolution of Advanced Levels

The design of AS level examinations and syllabuses has encompassed all of the technical developments that have taken place since the GCE system was introduced in 1951. Not only were the first syllabuses considered to be poor and the essay — the predominant form of assessment — much criticized, doubts were also raised about the relative standards of the different Boards' examinations. As a result of all of these pressures, public examinations became an area of active research and most of the GCE Boards established their own research units whose main functions were to investigate new methods of assessment and to research into issues of comparability. Much of our understanding of how school examinations function has come from this work.

Concomitantly, teachers, both as individuals and in groups, came to play a very much larger part in the processes of curriculum and examination development. The 1960s saw something of a curriculum revolution and almost every subject came to have its own curriculum project, often associated with a special examination. Some of these project examinations became extremely successful, but all served to increase teachers' awareness of assessment issues which in turn led to improved examinations. Two consistent trends can be identified:

- a trend towards the clearer specification of what is to be taught and how it is to be taught — this is best exemplified in the A level common cores exercise;
- a trend towards a clearer specification of aims, objectives and outcomes to be expected from the courses of study — the current exercises to develop A level grade descriptions are examples.

As a result of all of these pressures, current A level syllabuses have increased in complexity — some have as many as seven separate components, and a large number of different ways of assessing a subject may be used. There has also been a tendency towards specialization, with particular methods of assessment becoming confined to single components or sections of components. The space required to write down an A level syllabus and to describe the examination has increased tenfold in thirty years.

The Higginson Report

It is possible to interpret the recommendations contained within the recent Higginson Report in the light of the trends already identified. The primary recommendation is one of structural change and a move from three A level courses to five 'streamlined' courses. This attempt at structural reform, like so many attempts that have gone before it, is unlikely to prove acceptable. Indeed, the Secretary of State for Education and Science appears already to have dismissed this aspect of the Report for the time being. Within the pages of the Higginson Report, there are, however, other recommendations for improving the syllabuses and outcomes of A and AS levels — examples of the evolutionary change identified above. These changes are, I believe, likely to influence the development of A level and AS level examinations over the next 10–20 years. Much as the National Criteria have done for GCSE, the Higginson Report has served to record some of the recent developments and to focus attention on future possibilities.

Some Practical Issues for Schools

Turning from the historical to the practical issues I shall now consider some of the effects that AS levels are producing. In the initial proposal for the AS level examinations (DES, 1984) it was suggested that it could be implemented without extra resources by the use of common A and AS level teaching. In *Better Schools* (DES, 1985) it was reported that the concept of common teaching was unlikely to prove popular with schools and colleges and might inhibit the introduction of the new examination. As AS levels have been developed the emphasis on common teaching has been reduced and in the annual report of the Secondary Examinations Council for 1986–87 the idea is even described as 'not ideal'.

As part of the NEEDS Project (New Examinations: Evaluation and Development in Schools) — a cooperative research project into the effects of the GCSE and AS levels which is being organized by the Institute of Education, University of London; the University of East Anglia; the University of London School·Examinations Board (ULSEB) and the London Education Authorities Group (LEAG) — the ULSEB Research Officers have been undertaking surveys and case study visits to schools and colleges. The purpose being, firstly, to assess the impact of the new examination upon students, teachers, styles of teaching and school organization and, secondly, to identify the variety of timetable strategies which arise as AS levels are introduced. So far, it has been possible to identify six strategies being used to implement the examination.

(i) Separate A and AS Level Courses

Current thinking would seem to indicate separate A and AS level teaching is the most appropriate model but, at the present time when most schools are fully involved with the final stages of the first GCSE examinations, it is only the sixth form colleges, tertiary colleges and the largest secondary schools that seem able to contemplate separate courses in more than one or two subjects.

The number of separate AS level courses that have been introduced by a single centre varies widely from one to eighteen.

(ii) Vertical Division of the A Level Course

A number of schools and colleges are trying to teach both levels of the examination without extra resources by making a vertical division of the A level syllabus. They are seeking to teach A level for n (usually 8) periods per week with the AS level students attending $n/2$ of them. The difficulties of this approach are fairly obvious and it can, of course, only be implemented when the A level syllabus is capable of division in this way. Like later strategies it requires a very high degree of curriculum planning by the teachers.

The success of this strategy must depend to a very large extent upon the A or AS level syllabuses involved.

(iii) Horizontal Division of the A Level Course

Many schools and colleges are attempting to teach A and AS levels by having the AS level students attend for relevant blocks of A level work (modules). Once again, this model requires a very high degree of academic planning especially where students may be taking more than one AS level in the same timetable period.

(iv) Modular A and AS Level Courses

A new and interesting development pioneered by the Ridgeway School, Swindon, has been the introduction of modular A and AS level courses. The scheme differs from strategy (iii) above in its use of module assessments. We shall be hearing about the Ridgeway scheme in greater detail from the Headmaster tomorrow (see chapter 9 in this volume).

(v) AS Level in the First Year Sixth, and A Level in the Second Year Sixth

From the surveys undertaken it is clear that some schools and colleges are planning, from 1988 or 1989, to introduce one year AS level courses and then allow some of the successful students to proceed to an A level in the second year (shades of Q and F?). While his strategy is not within the general spirit of the examination, taking AS levels after one year is certainly not precluded. Such a pattern may well appear in mathematics, and some other subjects, where it has become traditional for students to progress from O to AO and then to A levels. Indeed, some AS level syllabuses have been devised with this in mind.

(vi) AS Levels Without Equivalent A Levels

Some schools and colleges have already introduced or intend to introduce AS level courses because they do not possess the resources to create full A levels in these subjects. Similarly, where falling rolls are putting full A levels in jeopardy, AS levels offer opportunities for maintaining subjects within the sixth form curriculum.

Other Strategies

One of the great strengths of the AS level system appears to be in the flexibility that it offers to schools and colleges. In introducing AS levels some schools and colleges are adopting mixed strategies rather than relying upon any single approach identified above.

The provision of AS level courses has been influenced by the development of the GCSE and many respondents to our survey have indicated their intention to defer the implementation of AS levels until the first GCSE candidates enter the sixth form. As part of another of the NEEDS studies, which is assessing the impact of the GCSE upon A and AS level courses, we have found that many schools and colleges are concerned about progress from 16+ to 18+ work. The belief exists that some GCSE candidates may not be sufficiently familiar with the sixth form approach to choose their subjects. To further require them to select between A and AS level courses is viewed by some as unrealistic. To overcome this particular problem one or two schools are experimenting with a common start to A and AS level courses, with differentiation following after the first month or half term of sixth form work.

Further Research

As part of the NEEDS Project we shall be monitoring the impact of the GCSE and AS levels, including the impact that the former may have upon the sixth form. In the next academic year we shall proceed to evaluations of the strategies that I have identified, and the others that may appear. We hope to disseminate results of this work to schools and colleges through a series of NEEDS papers which will be distributed through the regular mailings of the LEAG and ULSEB.

References

DEPARTMENT OF EDUCATION AND SCIENCE, (1980), *Examinations 16–18: A Consultative Paper*, London HMSO.

DEPARTMENT OF EDUCATION AND SCIENCE, (1984), *AS Levels: Proposals by the Secretaries of State for Education and Science and Wales for a Broader Curriculum for A-level Students*, London, HMSO.

DEPARTMENT OF EDUCATION AND SCIENCE, (1985), *Better Schools*, DES/Welsh Office, (Cmnd. 9469), London, HMSO.

M. Kingdon

DEPARTMENT OF EDUCATION AND SCIENCE, (1988), *Advancing A levels: Report of a Committee appointed by the Secretary of State for Education and Science and the Secretary of State for Wales*, (The Higginson Report), London, HMSO.

KEOHANE, K. (Chairman) (1979), 'Proposals for a Certificate of Extended Education', (CMND 7755), London, HMSO.

THE SECONDARY EXAMINATIONS COUNCIL (1987), *Annual Report 1986–7*, The Council.

Chapter 2

AS Levels and the Universities

Clive Wake

The last time I spoke in this theatre was at a similar schools occasion, except that at that time I was talking to your students. Kent runs a very successful modern languages day each year, and this is one of the places that is filled with people wanting to hear about French literature. I spoke to them on that occasion about Victor Hugo's plays. Quite a different topic this morning.

What I want to do is give you a descriptive account of what we in the Standing Conference on University Entrance (SCUE) have been trying to do in relation to AS levels and what we believe the universities intend to do about them. Some of you will have heard what I am about to say before. I constantly meet people I've addressed at previous conferences. Please forgive me if there is any repetition today. I do find that the information I have to give does bear repetition because there is a fair amount of ignorance about the universities' intentions — as emerges from the discussions at the conferences I attend and also in the educational press. I shall approach my topic from two angles: I want to talk first of all about the acceptance of AS levels by the universities and then I shall say a few words about AS levels and broadening, particularly from the point of view of the universities.

Initial Response of Universities

Let me, like Dr Kingdon, begin with a little history by way of background to the acceptance of AS levels by the universities. The universities came into the debate on broadening the curriculum with N and F and earned a very poor reputation by rejecting them. When I joined it, SCUE was still smarting from the criticism that had come its way about the universities' lack of support for the N and F proposals. When the DES published its proposals for AS levels, SCUE went out to the universities to find out how precisely they would react to this new initiative. Their response was overwhelmingly positive. All universities agreed that they would go along with the adoption of AS levels and that they would incorporate them into their entry requirements. There were a lot of variations. Universities individually have their own ideas on almost everything and running SCUE gives you some idea of the complexity of their entrance requirements when looked at across the country as a whole. Sometimes one is overcome by the impossibility of getting the universities to agree on a single course of action; but they did come together in their agreement about AS levels and their incorporation into entry requirements even if they went their different ways in the detailed application.

It also emerged very clearly from the universities' response that there was a considerable sensitivity on their part to the difficulties the schools and colleges (particularly the schools) would face with the introduction of AS levels. First of all, they recognized that there would be resource problems, and that the DES was not proposing to make extra resources available for the introduction of AS levels. Secondly, they also realized that there were many changes in the secondary curriculum already in the pipeline, indeed actively occurring. There was the GCSE in particular, which was taking off at that time, and of course TVEI. So there were two particular problems, resources and the multiple pressures of change on the schools. As a result of this, in responding formally to the DES, SCUE said that the universities would not for the time being make AS levels a compulsory element in their entry requirements. This did cause a certain amount of dismay among people outside the universities who supported AS levels and who were pleased that we had taken a stand, but who also felt that the universities should make AS levels a compulsory part of their entrance requirements to ensure their success. However we could not make AS levels compulsory while resources in the schools were not up to it and while there would, for some time, be many schools that would not be able to offer AS levels. So no compulsion.

From the outset SCUE envisaged a gradual development, a gradual uptake of AS levels. We were not at all surprised therefore at the low numbers coming forward for the first entry. Indeed we were pleased to see that they were as large as they were. And the uptake anticipated for the second year by the examining boards and the DES is even greater than we ourselves expected it to be at this stage, back in 1984. So, as far as we are concerned, the uptake is going well and we anticipate that it will continue to go well, particularly if we in the universities can get our act together and if we can respond to your particular needs in the schools and colleges.

SCUE: The First Leaflet

So, the universities welcomed AS levels and promised to incorporate them into their entrance requirements but, given the history, who could trust the universities on an issue like this? You certainly did not. It was important therefore that we should make a stand, and make it clear what we were going to do. So what SCUE did first of all was to produce an initial publication called *AS Levels and University Entrance*, which appeared in November 1986. I did not bring one with me this morning, but I am sure that most of you will have seen it, a blue A5 leaflet with a smiling face on the front of it: cheerful youngster entering the portals of AS levels, that's the way to sell things these days. In fact, I have a secret to tell you: he wasn't a university student, he was a polytechnic student. Our designer blissfully ignored the binary line. Anyway, behind that cheerful face we included all the statements we had collected from individual universities as to what they were going to do about AS levels. It was all entrance-requirements gobbledegook in a typical university way, so a lot of it was not as intelligible as we would have liked it to have been. But it was what the universities themselves said they were going to do, and we quite deliberately did not interfere with their own statements because we wanted to be able to hold them to their commitment.

What emerged from that first leaflet was that all universities would continue to require the basic two A levels, which was what was originally agreed in 1984: when we responded to the DES consultation we said that two A levels would remain for the time being the basis for entry into university. For the purposes of the general requirement, the universities said it would be possible to offer AS levels in place of O levels/GCSEs. This was not intended as a diminution of the importance of AS levels by giving them the same status as O levels or the GCSE; it was simply an alternative to the O level/GCSE option in the general requirement at a time when two A levels remained the basic requirement. As far as course entry requirements were concerned, most departments said at that stage they would accept two AS levels for a third A level. And in many cases, the universities very helpfully listed in some detail the courses for which this would be possible. As we pointed out in the introduction to that leaflet, the situation was one in which the universities' attitudes were evolving. It was a developing, not a static situation because we were faced with the eternal problem with the universities that I have already mentioned: their tendency to make up their minds individually.

SCUE: The Revised Leaflet

So we produced a revised edition of this leaflet in September 1987, less than a year after the first edition. This revised edition showed, as we expected, some significant changes in the position of the universities. As far as the general requirement was concerned, it showed a considerably increased flexibility. The Vice-Chancellor has already pointed out that in this year's edition of *University Entrance* you will find that a number of universities will now accept AS levels in place of one or both the required A levels for the purposes of general entry requirement. That is a major step forward, but of course (and I'll be quite frank with you) it is an illusion since it has at this stage no practical effect: it is the course entry requirement which is crucial and to date it is not possible to gain entry to any but a few courses by offering AS levels in place of one or both of the two basic A levels. But we are working on it, and I suspect there will be a shift in this direction in the not too distant future. As far as course entry requirements are concerned, there was a great increase in the number of courses that would accept AS levels in place of the third A level. It was particularly important to get Cambridge to amend its original statement on the acceptance of AS levels for entry to their science courses. Some of you wrote to us or phoned us after the first edition of the leaflet appeared complaining that while Cambridge made such a negative stance on the science side, no-one was going to be interested in AS levels. I do think that was an exaggeration, but it was nevertheless an important factor. We went back to Cambridge and urged them to reconsider their position. And you will see, if you compare the two editions, that the wording of the Cambridge entry changed quite significantly for the second edition.

We always knew that the second edition of *AS Levels and University Entrance* would be the last time we would make use of that particular means of promulgating the universities' position on the new examination. From now on, starting with the second edition of *University Entrance: The Official Guide* (published 1 June 1988), we shall be indicating the individual universities' position on AS levels in the Guide. If you have it already, you may have noticed that we go into some detail: not only do we set out the general entry requirement in terms of AS levels but we also show the acceptance of AS levels course by course. If you look at it from the statistical point of view, you will find that 98 per cent of all university courses (there are some 9000 courses listed in the book) now accept AS levels in place of the third A level. There is just a very small number of science courses where it is still not possible to offer AS levels; you can find out which these are from *University Entrance*.

Specified A Levels

There is a particular problem with regard to AS levels and their future which it is up to us in the universities to sort out. That is the problem of named A levels. Where an A level is specified for course entry, and particularly where more than one A level is specified for course entry, there is an inevitable reduction in the options that your students will have in applying for a place in higher education, because of the kind of choices that have to be made to ensure that options can be kept open. I'll give you an example. We had a letter from a 16-year-old saying that he wanted to take AS levels, and could we advise him as to how this could be done. He had two very different possibilities in mind for higher education. When I looked at the universities' entrance requirements, it became perfectly clear that he could not take AS levels, because in order to keep his options open for the two courses he had in mind he had to take three particular A levels. I give you this example to make the problem clear to you. Until it is sorted out, AS levels cannot be a free and ready option for the majority of sixth-formers. SCUE's job, then, is to get the universities to make AS levels as interchangeable with A levels as possible. That is to say, to minimize the number of specified A levels. We have been writing to the universities about this and we will continue to press them on this issue.

There are two particular kinds of specified A levels. There is the specified third A level, that is a situation where three A levels are specified for entry to a particular course. This is virtually eliminated. Our latest success was with the medical schools, a very important step because so many applicants wish to keep medicine as an option; it may just be a vague dream, but while it's there, they want to be able to keep the option open, and it is important to make it possible for them to do so. So, until medicine conceded the third A level and allowed AS levels to be offered in its place, your hands were tied and ours were tied too. In this connection, I can tell you that we had a meeting with the General Medical Council during the course of last week to discuss a major conference they are organizing early next year to consider the implications of the changes in secondary education for the medical curriculum. This includes AS levels. The conference will be aimed at medical school teachers and particularly at admissions tutors.

The second problem regarding specified A levels is the situation where you have A levels specified for the first or second A level. In other words, up to two of three A levels are specified. While there is a large number of these, the difficulties about keeping options open remain. As the Vice-Chancellor pointed out when he introduced the conference, universities like Kent have begun to accept that AS levels can replace required A levels in this category, and he cited the example of chemistry at Kent. If you study *University Entrance*, you will find that other universities are beginning to follow this example. But this is still the area where we have the greatest amount of work to do. If you go back to *University Entrance*, and get your calculators out, you will find that so far only about 15 per cent of the courses specifying one or two A level subjects will allow the substitution of AS levels, very different from the third specified A level picture of 98 per cent. We would like to see a readiness on the part of the sciences to allow AS levels to be substituted as often as possible for named A levels. We have been working very hard on the engineers about their A level physics requirement and we are beginning to make headway. It is likely that in a year or two, especially if the examining boards can introduce core content into the AS level, AS physics will be acceptable for entry into engineering in place of the A level.

We would also like this to happen in humanities. This University, like many others, insists that you must have A level English in order to enter degree courses in English. Personally I do not believe that is necessary and I do hope that universities that still have this requirement will have another look at it with a view to dropping it. The same applies to modern languages, a much trickier problem, but I do believe that there could be much more flexibility in this area too.

Admissions Tutors

From what I've said to you already, you must be aware that we have made a considerable effort to ensure that the universities accept AS levels and incorporate them at all levels into their requirements. I would like to say a bit more about the particular kinds of strategies that we have adopted, and I shall refer particularly to one problem which I know does bother the schools and colleges: the actual response admissions tutors are likely to make to applicants offering AS levels when they begin to come forward next autumn.

Firstly, SCUE has mounted a campaign to familiarize universities with AS levels which is quite unprecedented. At no time in my experience as a university teacher have university teachers and admissions tutors been so pressed to take on board a change of this kind, and I should be very surprised if there is an admissions tutor anywhere in the university system who has not by now heard of AS levels and been made aware of the importance of taking them seriously. It *has* been an unprecedented campaign and I do believe that we have got the message across to university people to an extent that would not have been possible had we simply said in 1985 — 'OK, AS levels are now to be implemented, over to you, the schools and colleges. Produce the students and we'll see what happens then'. We felt in SCUE that we had a duty to you to ensure that the universities fulfilled their commitment to AS levels, and we have tried to show that we recognize this by conducting this campaign within the universities.

In addition to producing the two leaflets I have mentioned, we got together with the Council for National Academic Awards (CNAA), the SCDC and the SEC to produce a very successful leaflet, entitled *Current developments in school curriculum and examinations* (1987), aimed at teachers in higher education. It told them about the changes taking place in the secondary curriculum. It was brief and to the point, and knowing that we were dealing with extremely busy people, we even highlighted the bits that were of particular importance. That leaflet was, as I say, a very considerable success and was devoured by the institutions. In fact, it has also been much in demand outside higher education, so much so that we are hoping, if we can raise the funds, to produce a revised edition next year aimed at a wider audience. On that occasion, we intend that you yourselves should receive copies.

Another aspect of our activities was the decision to take up the Secretary of State's invitation in *Better Schools* that SCUE should be involved in some way in the preparation of AS level syllabuses. We did this by joining forces with CNAA, that is, by bringing together the two sectors of higher education. We set up joint subject panels to look at the draft syllabuses as the boards produced them. These panels have been working away over the past two years, looking at a constant stream of syllabuses in draft form, commenting on them and sending the comments back to the boards, copying the comments to SEC, and getting back from the boards comments on our comments. We have been very pleased at the extent to which our comments have been taken on board. We did not assume that they would all be adopted; there must be differences of opinion in matters of this kind. We undertook this exercise because we wanted to be able to say to higher education that the AS syllabuses had been looked at from their point of view and had been found satisfactory.

In instructing our panels what to do we asked them to pay particular attention to four factors. Firstly, we asked them to take account of the GCSE, and to bear in mind that clearly the GCSE must have its effect on AS levels as well. Secondly, we felt it was particularly important in this first run of AS level syllabuses that our panels should do their best to ensure that the weighting of content was about right. In our view, it is not possible in most cases simply to take an A level syllabus and cut it in half. Half an A level syllabus in one subject taught alongside half a syllabus in another subject might well add up to more than an A level in one of the subjects. We felt that great care would have to be taken to ensure that the content of the AS level syllabuses was not excessive and did not make excessive demands on those taking them. The effect of this happening would be to discourage people from taking AS levels. Thirdly, we asked our panels to give positive encouragement to the development of new kinds of syllabus, to syllabuses that indicated a readiness on the part of examining boards to take the opportunity to innovate. For a variety of reasons, it was not possible for the boards to develop too many innovative syllabuses, but there is a good sprinkling of them, and we were very pleased to see them — some of the mathematics syllabuses in particular, and one or two of those in languages. Finally, not related to AS levels specifically, but arising from a very strong point of policy with SCUE, we told our panels to have it quite clear in their minds as they scrutinized the syllabuses that higher education, and the universities in particular, should no longer appear to be imposing their will on the secondary curriculum. It is high time for this particular approach to cease. The universities are just one of a number of outlets for sixth-formers taking A levels.

In fact, as an extension of this last point, we would very much like to see access to A levels themselves widened, so that they will be attractive to a much broader range and to larger numbers of youngsters who may not necessarily wish to go on to higher education, who may seek other outlets in a society that places an ever higher premium on qualifications. We must therefore, in our view, develop a secondary curriculum which can take this into account. And, because we have rather a bad reputation in this respect, one thing we in the universities have to do is to contribute by ensuring that A and AS levels do not continue to be planned as if only universities have an interest in these qualifications.

I turn now to the question of the admissions tutors and their attitude to AS levels. Whenever I address gatherings of school and college teachers, this point always comes up. Can admissions tutors be trusted to implement the policies on AS levels laid down by their universities, faculties and departments? Everybody seems to know of an admissions tutor locked away somewhere in some university who has said he or she will not accept AS levels in spite of stated policy, and I can believe that such people might exist. Given the autonomy of individual university institutions, which within themselves have a very large measure of autonomy as between faculties and departments, it is extraordinarily difficult to make sure that everyone is towing the party line on admissions procedures, whatever you do. We are hopeful that our own campaign will minimize the possibility that many admissions tutors will, in fact, ignore policy on the implementation of AS levels. The point to bear in mind here is that universities have stated in black and white in their prospectuses and in *University Entrance* what they propose to do, and their admissions tutors do have an obligation to fulfil the statements their institutions have made in writing. If in your experience any admissions tutor does not appear to be doing so, you must raise it with the university, and if necessary make an issue of it. It is important that we in the universities do in fact fulfil the promises we make in this as in other matters; we are under an obligation to provide the service we have guaranteed. If we do not ensure that we do so in connection with AS levels, it will be nothing less than a confidence trick that we are playing on the community. I attended the last UCCA Admissions Officers' Conference specifically to make this point, and I was very pleased with the very positive response I got when I made it even more strongly than I am making it to you now. So do make sure that we do as we promise.

Monitoring Progress

SCUE will be monitoring the progress of AS levels in the universities. There are many ways in which we can do this. One of these is by using the UCCA statistics. UCCA can produce a wide range of statistics, many of which are not published because they are not of interest to the general public. We shall be able to obtain statistics, for example, on the number of applicants who offered AS levels, the number who were made offers with AS levels, and the number who were accepted with AS levels. We will be able to compare these figures with the related figures for A levels and obtain quite a good picture of the way things are going. If anything untoward emerges, I hope you will accept my word that we shall take the matter up with the universities concerned.

As Offer Levels

On the admissions side, there is another point that is raised quite often by the schools — I imagine it is something on your minds as well — and that is the question of the level of the offers universities should make for AS levels. Should the same grades be asked or accepted or required for both AS levels and A levels? By and large this would have to be the case in order to have comparability. But we have warned the universities that this is a new examination and that there will be problems of comparison. By taking two AS levels in place of a third A level, a sixth-former may in some respects increase his or her workload, especially if the choice involves a contrasting AS level. It is not easy, if you are, say, a scientist but you are interested in languages or in literature, to take an AS level in a language or a literature and obtain exactly the same grade that might have been obtained if the choice had been a science subject. Unless the universities are prepared to be flexible about this, the extension of AS levels, particularly in terms of broadening, will not take place. It is therefore vitally important that they take this into account. Universities do however have their own problems about making lower offers for AS levels. Many see their prestige within the community as being reflected at least in part by the average points scores achieved by their applicants. There is a possibility that points scores will cease to be used formally as a performance indicator in the university system. I personally hope this will be the case, because not only in this area, but in other areas too, the use of points scores does distort the whole business of the entrance to universities.

While I am on the question of points scores, I could perhaps tell you how points scores will be used in relation to AS levels. We receive a lot of queries about this and there is a very simple answer. An AS level will have half the score of an A level. In order to make it easier to calculate, the present A level points will be doubled, so that you will have 10 for an A and so on. AS levels will have the same range of points as A levels do at the moment, so that you can tot A and AS levels up together and get a nice round figure with a maximum of 30. The total will then be divided by 2, for the purely practical reason that we need some sort of comparison with pre-AS level scores while we are going through the transition period. The essential point is that A and AS levels will be completely integrated for the purposes of establishing the points scores of applicants.

Finally, a few words about AS levels and broadening. AS levels are intended to broaden the curriculum. Many people are sceptical that they will in fact do so. There is a fundamental tendency for both students and their teachers to specialize unless they are not given a push in the opposite direction. What is quite likely to happen if we are not very careful is that sixth-formers will simply take four science subjects or four humanities subjects, instead of the three science subjects or three humanities subjects they take at the moment. In other words, the urge to specialize will be reinforced. There will be a bit of broadening within that specialization in the sense that the sixth-former will have a wider experience of particular subject areas, but this is not the kind of broadening that AS levels are intended to produce, as I understand it. We shall therefore need positively to encourage the development of contrasting AS levels. Not much progress has been made on this within the universities as yet. A number of departments do state that they will accept contrasting AS levels; some say more categorically that they would like to see applicants offering contrasting AS levels. We do know, for example, that engineers are very keen for their entrants to have taken an arts or social science subject in the sixth-form. In particular, they like them to have taken English or a language, and AS levels will provide a marvellous way of achieving this; sixth-formers can still take their three sciences and also take a fourth subject outside the science. I do happen to know, because I speak quite a lot to the engineers, that they are quite keen that this should happen.

A report on the growth of mixed A levels was published in 1987 by Alan Smithers and Pamela Robinson of Manchester University which showed that there has been a significant increase in the number of sixth-formers who are taking mixed A levels. There is clearly a kind of groundswell here, as it shows that a lot of young people are themselves anxious to broaden their studies. We are hoping very much that AS levels will encourage this development.

Implications for Universities

One last point. If we take forward the kinds of development that I was suggesting earlier on, especially the need to allow AS levels to be substituted for A levels in the same subject, the introduction of AS levels will have implications for the universities themselves in terms of the kind of students they are going to receive in the future. If you add to AS levels the fact that students will be applying to universities in a year or two having done the GCSE, that they will increasingly have taken A levels modified in the light of the GCSE, and that many of them will have followed a TVEI programme, you have a clutch of changes taking place in the secondary curriculum of which the universities must take account. In addition to that, there is the greater emphasis being placed on mature students and on the development of access courses. The Committee of Vice-Chancellors and Principals (CVCP) and SCUE therefore wrote some months ago to the universities outlining the nature of the changes taking place in the educational background of their applicants and advising them that they should look at their course structures and at their teaching methods to see in what ways they needed to be modified in the light of these developments. It is our belief that some quite fundamental modifications will be needed, and that the universities must get down to the work that has to be done now, and not leave it until entrants who have experienced this new curriculum start coming through and find themselves floundering in the first year of their university course. We have asked the universities to produce an initial progress report at the end of June 1988 and a summary of their reports will be published in the autumn. This summary will be intended specifically for yourselves, for the schools and for the colleges, so that you will know what the universities are doing and are planning to do to take account of the changes that are taking place in the secondary curriculum.

Discussion on chapters 1 and 2

Dr. Ingram It is now time to open up the discussion. The floor is open to anyone who wishes to ask a question or comment on any aspect covered — or indeed, not covered — during this morning's session.

Mr. Crossan Do you accept the need for a four year university course?

Dr. Ingram I think the simple answer to that is no. I suspect that is one of the reasons why the government turned down Higginson. I think the government's attitude would be that they cannot afford a four year course. Even if we felt strongly that there is such a need, I think the likelihood of getting it for university courses in the near future is very small. Following up Professor Wake's point, if students no longer have three A levels when they enter university we will need to give some thought to our courses, particularly our first year courses.

Mr. Langley I would find it very useful, I think, at this stage if someone could attempt to clarify the exact relationship between the examination boards and the universities. Taking a naive view, I found myself asking the question: 'What exactly is going on?' It seems that we have a new product (AS) on the market on which people like myself have to make a judgment, namely whether we wish to purchase this product for our clients. Yet at the same time we are being told that it is up to us to persuade the universities of the surrender value of this product, having first persuaded our students to acquire it. We are being invited to purchase it for our clients, even though there may be a strong possibility that quite a number of universities will not accept two AS levels.

Dr. Kingdon The relationship is a complex one. The universities and school examinations boards are hybrid organizations. They have similarities with university departments — because such are their origins — and with large international business organizations. The boards do not, for example, come under the UGC; they are fee earning organizations and have, like all such bodies, not to make a loss if they are to survive. The Higher School Certificate examinations were organized by universities for universities. Since the introduction of the GCE the situation is different. There has been a strong tendency for teachers — through membership of their professional associations — to have executive control of the examinations. So at the moment, the relationship between an examination board and the university with which it may be linked by name is an extremely complex one. The boards are, of course, aware of the very important fact that the qualifications they produce are used for a very large number of purposes other than university entrance. So, although the universities have a role to play in assisting in the development of GCE A and AS examinations, so do teachers, professional bodies and employers. It is a very complex process of checks and balances. Those who have ideas and are conversant with the examinations have numerous channels through which inputs can be made. Similarly bodies such as UCCA, SCUE and PCAS all have an input and the SEC has executive responsibility for approving syllabuses produced by the boards.

Dr. Ingram So there you are: the examination boards are not in the pocket of the universities as they once were.

Professor Wake Our own relations with the examining boards are exactly that kind, we don't tell the boards what they can do. We have to petition them, we have to tie up with them in a way that anybody else who has an interest in what they are producing has to do. Although many of them bear the names of a university, they are independent. So it is not a case of there being a closed circle of common interests. Often we disagree quite profoundly.

Dr. Ingram But you do have a kind of chicken and egg situation as far as AS is concerned. Universities are saying: 'Yes, we will accept them, but of course we want to see what kind of product comes through from the schools and the kinds of grades that are going to be obtained'. You in the schools are saying: 'Yes, but until we know what universities are going to do we don't know whether to take AS levels seriously'. There must be an 'act of faith' on both sides. We, in the universities, must believe that you, in the schools, are going to take us seriously and send us good students via AS levels, and you must believe that we will give due recognition to the qualification and willingly admit students possessing it into our courses. I think both of us do have to undertake an act of faith just at the moment. On our side I do not believe there is anything more that we can do at this stage. We have taken this very seriously, put out formal statements saying we will accept AS levels and as Professor Wake says, we have carried out a very considerable publicity campaign aimed at our own admissions officers pointing out that they really must take this qualification seriously. We would like you to tell us, and we do genuinely mean this, if you feel any university is not doing so. Write not only to that university, but to SCUE itself, because we do want to make sure that our proposals are followed up properly.

Mr. Langley It was very interesting to learn that 98 per cent of courses accept AS levels as the third A level, but I think we would feel that there is a real breakthrough when a large number of university courses begin to accept AS in place of the second A level.

Dr. Ingram Yes, I think that is a fair comment. Professor Wake will be working hard on that.

Dr. Kingdon There are perhaps two issues here. Firstly, that the success of AS levels is dependent upon the development of a cycle of confidence and the examination boards have an input to that cycle at several points, as do employers. Secondly, there is a general move towards broadening courses and AS levels are only a part of the process. A few years ago it was enough to think of university entrance as being an end in itself. But one of the things that I feel has been very important in helping to bring about AS levels has been the recognition of a broader education as something of value in itself as well as of value to employers. Employers like their employees to be adaptable. A large number of the country's most influential employers have endorsed AS levels.

We should also note that there are other thrusts for a broadening of courses and that these come from a variety of sources, schools, higher education, professional bodies and government itself. For example, the present government seems to take the view that the commercial viability of this country depends upon producing a work force that has adaptability, and that this has been constrained in the past at several levels by a curriculum that is too narrow.

Professor Wake This question of schools and colleges having to engage in an act of faith is one which I think we in the universities have got to try and understand. On the other hand you should understand that, in a sense, when one of your students applies for a university place, that itself is an act of faith, at least to some extent. He or she is still in the hands of an individual admissions tutor who may or may not like the particular combination of subjects your student is taking. Furthermore, it is very difficult to do anything about this. But on a more practical level, we have got to try and do everything we can to ensure that AS is accepted by admissions tutors. To this end we shall be monitoring the UCCA statistics, with a view to getting out a report on the first cohort of AS candidates. We shall then see whether or not the universities are meeting their commitment.

Dr. Ingram I think you will have every right to challenge us if the statistics do not match up with what we said we were going to do. Also you are certainly right when you imply that we have to persuade universities to accept AS levels in place of the second and first A level.

Question It may not be widely appreciated that many students have simply added one AS level to an already full programme. Is it possible to guarantee that the incorporation of the AS levels into the students' programme will not merely push up the admission standard?

Dr. Ingram Of course, they can take four or five A levels now if they want to, although in making that point I am not suggesting that it is wise for them to do so.

Professor Wake This development is one which a number of people have noted. I suspect that it is really the act of faith problem, that until people are really sure that AS levels will be accepted within the bounds of the traditional three A level situation, AS levels will tend very often to be added on. This development does worry us considerably. In the very early days a number of schools put the question to me: 'Will the universities now go over to the requirement of three A levels plus one AS level?' I must stress this is not something we would like to see happen, and I have no evidence whatsoever that this is becoming a development in the universities. Obviously, as the Vice-Chancellor suggests, there is the situation whereby some students come forward with four A levels and even more at the moment. And no doubt an additional AS level instead of an additional A level would be very attractive to a lot of people. Indeed, the very existence of AS might increase the number of students who might take something extra. But, I think the emphatic point to make is that we have got to resist — and you have got to do it as much as we have — the notion that entry into higher education is going to become more expensive in terms of entry qualifications.

Dr. Kingdon The examination boards have already provided a wide range of AS syllabuses and the development of others continues. Of course, we have to recognize that there is considerable expense involved in developing syllabuses. The examination boards are therefore keen to understand and learn the effects that their syllabuses are having, how they are being taught and how they are used.

We are aware that one of the main problems in schools is that of resources — or rather the lack of them — to teach AS syllabuses. At the moment schools are tending to choose AS syllabuses from within the conventional (core) subject areas. Teachers are being cautious; they do not want to disadvantage their students by making the wrong choices at this early stage in the history of AS.

I think one of the things that has come out of the rejection of the structural proposals of the Higginson Committee is the fact that even within the few weeks that have elapsed since the publication of its report there has been a great swell of interest in AS levels — indeed the attendance at this conference might be partly indicative of this. If the volume of enquiries we have been having recently, both on the technical side and on the syllabus development side, are anything to go by, it would appear that teachers are now more confident that AS levels will go ahead and are not going to be replaced by some modified or revised system as a result of the Higginson proposals. Perhaps people will now be a little more adventurous and try the types of structures that Professor Wake has been proposing.

Dr. Ingram When Sir Keith Joseph originally asked us to look at AS levels, he certainly hoped that we would insist that one of them should be in a contrasting subject, but we decided that in the end we really could not insist on this because it would require extra resources. If we had insisted on a contrasting AS level, as we would have liked to have done for academic reasons, we would have been penalizing the schools who just had not got the resources to do it. This is still one of the major questions; it is really a resource question which ought to be put to Mr. Robert Jackson tomorrow. It is certainly desirable that we achieve more in the way of contrasting AS levels.

Dr. Kingdon AS development has been constrained by a lack of resources. There are various views about the form that AS syllabuses ought to take. The design of these began at about the same time as the A level common core exercise and there was considerable support for equating AS levels with the common core of A levels. This would, in my view, give rise to a fairly stodgy, uninteresting and rather boring syllabus. The introduction of AS levels provided us with an opportunity to re-examine the role that individual subjects have in the sixth form curriculum. In practice it has provided an opportunity to do something new in the form of a coherent two year course for students who may or may not have done GCSE. Coherence and integrity are important criteria which the SEC has looked for when approving new AS syllabuses. They have been careful to ensure that an AS syllabus is not just an A level syllabus chopped in two.

Mr. Shearn   Coming back to the act of faith. What is the admissions tutor going to do when confronted by two candidates, one with three traditional A levels and the other with two A levels plus two AS levels? Is he going to credit the latter with having pursued a broader curriculum and relax the offer level to take account of this? Or is he going to attach greater weight to A levels than to ASs?

Professor Wake   It is an almost impossible question to answer without trying to pretend that there isn't a problem. There clearly is a problem here, and it illustrates the seriousness of the act of faith situation. We have, as I said, tried to impress it on universities that they may well have to make lower offers to people on AS levels, particularly when they are contrasting. All we can do at this stage, I'm afraid, is monitor the situation. And we will do so. But I take the point of the illustration very seriously indeed.

Dr. Ingram   When we sent out the first AS levels booklet some university departments responded quite positively by stating they would welcome contrasting AS levels instead of a third A level. So hopefully students will get extra credit for having done such AS levels. We will have to wait and see.

Mr. Boatman   Given the risks that our students take and the resource costs that we face in putting on these courses I wish I could feel more reassured by what I have heard this morning.

Professor Wake   It is almost impossible to answer that kind of statement. I would hope that the schools which have already introduced AS levels, knowing these problems, would perhaps comment. Because they have taken this risk, they have acted on and taken that act of faith and their students will soon be interviewed and screened by universities for entrance.

Dr. Ingram   Does anyone want to comment on why they started AS levels?

Mr. Hunt We intend to start AS levels from next September, and we are also worried about this act of faith. So we wrote round to 130 admissions tutors this time last year asking what their advice would be. Now on this very open ended question we got about eighty-five replies of which about half were 'let us wait and see', and the rest were really quite positive. The kinds of response we got were sufficiently encouraging for us to go ahead.

Dr. Kingdon The time scale for the development of this examination has been incredibly short. In 1989 it will have been just five years from first proposal to first exam. Now that is quick by any standards. It does mean that for many aspects of the new examination there has not been research and development, the trials that would usually accompany a development of this magnitude — the GCSE is another example. It means that in terms of AS level standards there are still issues that are unresolved; in the examination boards' presentations this afternoon we will be hearing more about AS level standards and their relationship with A level standards. I am sure you will all be reassured to know that this is something which is being tackled by the GCE boards on a cooperative basis. I know the boards are often commercial competitors but over technical issues they are colleagues. For about twenty years they have cooperated on technical research and the Research Officers of the boards are giving active consideration to the issues. In the autumn we will be preparing a series of papers in which will be discussed the issue of common standards of performance on common A and AS level examination components. For example, what will be the likely results of a student with two AS level passes which are complementary as against a student with one contrasting and one complementary pass. All I can do at the moment is reassure you that these matters are under active consideration.

Dr. Ingram Could I just give one final comment on this. If you believe in admission by a points system, you are home and dry because we promised that AS levels would go into the points system in exactly the way Professor Wake described earlier. Hence, if your student is going to be accepted by a university just on the points score, this will guarantee that AS level has its correct weighting, equal to half an A level. So that is some kind of guarantee. This should be some reassurance to you, although a lot of us believe that it is not just points that count in university entrance.

Section II
Progress on AS Levels

Chapter 3

The Case for Breadth

Paul Scruton

Destination of A Level Students

I have brought some slides which tell us a bit about what people do after they have gained their A levels. I think they illustrate the case for breadth in A level studies. And by breadth in A level studies I include the sort of breadth provided by AS as well as a sort of breadth that I believe needs to be provided within A level itself. The slides are based on figures that are a little out of date, because for some reason it does seem to take a long time to compile educational statistics. But I don't think this invalidates them: if anything, recent trends add to their force. The two sources are the DES 10 per cent sample of school-leavers in the academic year 1984–85, and some figures compiled by the Schools Liaison Committee of the Association of Graduate Careers Advisory Services.

History

Figure 1 is concerned with the subject history. The vertical bar represents all those who have succeeded in getting an A level in history. It is divided up to show the intended destinations of those getting the A level. The part of the bar shaded in various depths of grey shows the proportion that we know went on to take a degree course in a known subject at a university or other higher education institution. The white part of the bar shows the proportion that had intended either to take some other kind of course, or to go straight into employment; and it also includes the 'don't knows'. So the proportion that is grey gives us a rough idea of one sort of

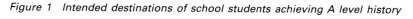

Figure 1   Intended destinations of school students achieving A level history

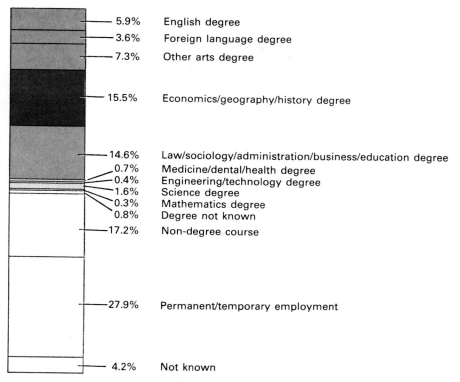

5.9%   English degree

3.6%   Foreign language degree

7.3%   Other arts degree

15.5%   Economics/geography/history degree

14.6%   Law/sociology/administration/business/education degree
0.7%   Medicine/dental/health degree
0.4%   Engineering/technology degree
1.6%   Science degree
0.3%   Mathematics degree
0.8%   Degree not known
17.2%   Non-degree course

27.9%   Permanent/temporary employment

4.2%   Not known

participation rate in higher education. You can see that over half who get A level history go on to take some sort of degree course.

What do the different shades of grey mean? I have used the darkest grey to represent those students who transferred into the same subject area when they left school: in this case they took history as an A level and then also took some sort of humanities subject as a degree course. The medium grey represents candidates who took a degree course in a subject related to history, like languages, other arts subjects or law. I have used the lightest grey to represent those students who took a degree course in a subject very different from history, like engineering. Of course we could argue about what subjects are 'related' and which are 'different' but that doesn't matter: the different shades give some idea of the overall picture but you can make your own judgments about how related the subjects are. We should not of course expect history — or indeed humanities — to be necessarily the dominant degree course for these students. After all, those entering higher education will typically have taken two other A levels in subjects other than history.

Chemistry

Figure 2 shows a similar story but is about chemistry. This time the vertical bar represents all those who have succeeded in getting an A level in chemistry and again it is divided up to show their intended destinations. The grey parts of the bar once again show the proportions that were intending to do a degree course in some known subject, with the white part of the bar again showing the proportions set to take some other kind of course or to go straight into employment or for whom destination was not known. You can see immediately that a greater proportion of the bar is grey than

Figure 2   *Intended destinations of school students achieving A level chemistry*

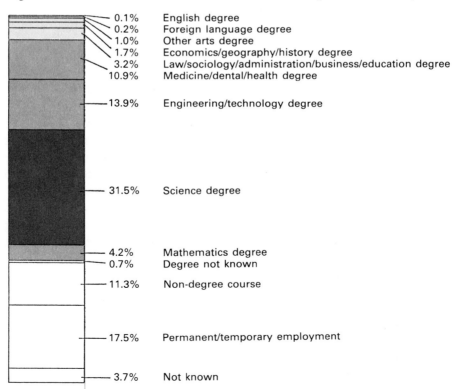

0.1%	English degree
0.2%	Foreign language degree
1.0%	Other arts degree
1.7%	Economics/geography/history degree
3.2%	Law/sociology/administration/business/education degree
10.9%	Medicine/dental/health degree
13.9%	Engineering/technology degree
31.5%	Science degree
4.2%	Mathematics degree
0.7%	Degree not known
11.3%	Non-degree course
17.5%	Permanent/temporary employment
3.7%	Not known

for history. In fact over 70 per cent of those with chemistry A level were about to follow degree courses.

Once again, dark grey represents those students who transferred into the same subject area when they left school: in this case having taken chemistry as an A level they were also set to take some sort of science degree course. Notice that this dark grey portion is large compared with that for history: it is large both as a proportion of the students getting the A level and as a proportion of those going on to degree courses. Medium grey again shows candidates who took a degree course in a subject related to chemistry, like engineering or medicine while light grey represents those students set for a degree course in a subject very different from chemistry, like English. Overall you can see that a lot of people who succeeded in chemistry were intending to go on to do a subject like it, or related to it.

Figure 3 is also about chemistry but it shows the next stage on. It considers those who stay with chemistry and become graduates in that subject. The left-hand bar is broken down to show broadly what people do when they graduate. It shows there is a roughly equal division into permanent UK employment, further academic study, and other destinations. If we take the grey section of the bar — that is the one on UK employment — and look for a bit more detail about what sorts of jobs people did we get the bar on the right-hand side. About a third of these go into scientific work and another tenth or so go into scientific support work. But science is not the destination for the majority. Instead they go into jobs where it would seem some understanding of institutions would be valuable — of how they have evolved, of the cultures which exist within them and impinge upon them; they go into jobs where some understanding of operational theory and above all the ability to communicate would clearly seem to be of some importance.

The case for breadth is starting to show itself: as educators we can ask what we provide at present beyond 16+ as a broadening experience for those whom we educate to a high level specializing in science. You might have read an article by Professor Ted Wragg in the *Guardian* a couple of weeks ago. He pointed out that if you fall ill in many European countries the chances are that you will find a doctor who speaks English, because many students heading for the professions take a language up to 18, 19 or beyond. 'Pity the poor Frenchman picking up some ailment here', says Ted Wragg. 'Unless the pen of his aunt is manifestly stuck in his left earhole, the doctor who treats him, having waved a cheery goodbye to

Figure 3   First destinations of chemistry graduates 1982

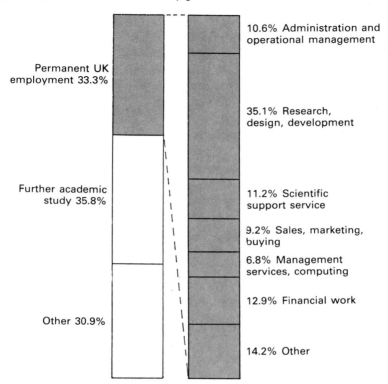

Permanent UK
employment 33.3%

10.6% Administration and
operational management

35.1% Research,
design, development

Further academic
study 35.8%

11.2% Scientific
support service

9.2% Sales, marketing,
buying

6.8% Management
services, computing

12.9% Financial work

Other 30.9%

14.2% Other

schoolboy French at 16, will probably have to resort to sign language.'

The case for science specialists continuing with modern languages is strong. One department of government constantly reminds us in its advertising that 1992 beckons. Yet a lack of properly located linguistic skills will mean that opportunities for access to technical, industrial and commercial literature and contacts will be lost.

Modern Languages

Figure 4 shows what was about to happen to school students who obtained A level in a modern language. The same shades-of-grey code is applied. This provides a corollary to what I have just said. It shows that among the lightest grey (unrelated) subjects only a small number of those studying modern languages — no more than about

Figure 4 Intended destinations of school students achieving A level in a modern language

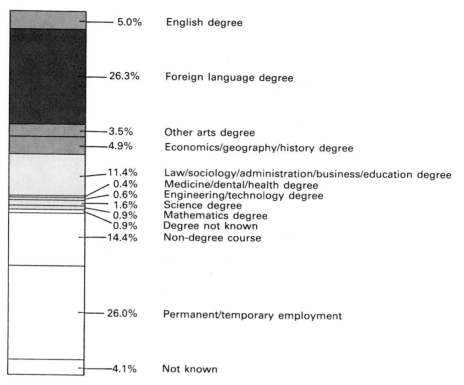

— 5.0%   English degree

— 26.3%   Foreign language degree

—3.5%   Other arts degree
—4.9%   Economics/geography/history degree

—11.4%   Law/sociology/administration/business/education degree
— 0.4%   Medicine/dental/health degree
— 0.6%   Engineering/technology degree
— 1.6%   Science degree
—0.9%   Mathematics degree
—0.9%   Degree not known
—14.4%   Non-degree course

— 26.0%   Permanent/temporary employment

—4.1%   Not known

3 per cent — are among our future scientists and technologists. Almost half of those who go on to a degree course continue with modern languages: that is high compared with other subjects.

Figure 5 shows the first destinations of those with modern languages degrees. A significant number go into teacher training, which is not true of the chemists. And quite a few take overseas employment, as you might expect.

As I did with the chemists I have taken the number going into UK employment (the grey section in the left-hand bar) and rebased it to 100 per cent in the right-hand bar to show a bit more of the detail. If you thought that most people with a modern languages degree go looking for jobs in publishing or libraries or the BBC you'd be wrong. As you can see, the great majority went into administration, marketing, management of one sort or another, or financial work. What I find striking about these areas of work is

Figure 5   First destinations of modern foreign languages graduates 1982

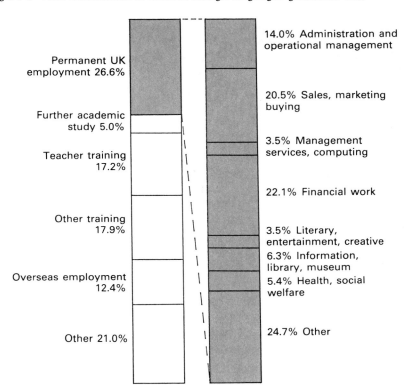

that they all involve basic skills of numeracy. So I ask the same sort of question as before: what do we do beyond 16 to build mathematical understanding of those who specialize in languages or other arts subjects and then do work of this kind? How do we feel about having administrators who have been educated to become talented arts-specialists but who have no grasp of scientific or technical matters?

I realize that some of you may be thinking that I have only used arguments of a utilitarian and prevocational kind in arguing for breadth. I do not want to apologize for using those sorts of arguments but equally I do not want to leave you with the impression that those are the only arguments for breadth: equally forceful arguments can be based on the educational entitlement of the individual. An understanding of the humanities simply broadens the horizons of someone whose professional aims centre on, say, medicine. Some knowledge of, say, cosmology — while useful to only a few — no doubt has a sobering and humanizing effect upon us all.

Issues of broadening raise some points about how courses ought to be designed. AS level is the subject of this conference and AS level is the means for broadening available to us at present. Although the standard of AS level is to be formally linked to that of A level, I do not think that this means that AS syllabuses must be produced by a halving of present A levels. It is easy to see why halved A levels have appeared among the first AS levels and have been tolerated as AS levels: it is because many schools and colleges find it impossible to mount AS levels without some parallel teaching of A and AS students. But I suspect that the greatest educational effect will be achieved by those syllabuses and courses that have been developed specially with broadening in view. For example, in some modern language AS level syllabuses the stress has moved away from skill in writing the language towards greater fluency in listening and speaking. Such AS levels are intended for science specialists. Since AS levels are required to have an equivalence to A level such steps stand in danger of being attacked as implying a reduction in the quality of A level. I do not think this is the case: what has taken place is a qualitative change in the skills assessed, not a lowering of standards.

Mathematics

Figure 6 is about mathematics, and I think it illustrates further the need to redesign courses and syllabuses with broadening intentions in mind. Again it shows the intended destinations of those who have obtained an A level in the subject. As you can see, about a quarter of those who enter higher education take degree subjects such as English, foreign languages, arts, humanities, law, social science, administration, business or education. Little more than one-tenth of those entering higher education take a mathematical subject as a degree course.

We can speculate on why so few who are successful in mathematics at A level — and remember that some of those will have obtained double mathematics at A level — why so few go on to the subject in higher education. Is it because specialist degree courses are unattractive? Or is it because mathematics by its nature fits people so well for so many other things? It is after all the most celebrated of service subjects, and as figure 6 shows, a lot of people

Figure 6   Intended destinations of school students achieving A level mathematics

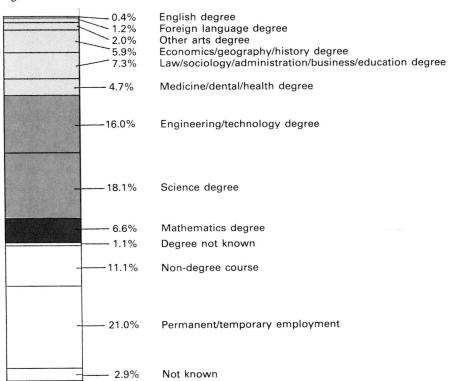

0.4%	English degree
1.2%	Foreign language degree
2.0%	Other arts degree
5.9%	Economics/geography/history degree
7.3%	Law/sociology/administration/business/education degree
4.7%	Medicine/dental/health degree
16.0%	Engineering/technology degree
18.1%	Science degree
6.6%	Mathematics degree
1.1%	Degree not known
11.1%	Non-degree course
21.0%	Permanent/temporary employment
2.9%	Not known

will be using their mathematics in the science, engineering and technology degrees that they go on to take.

Syllabus Design

This raises the whole question of who should have influence on the design of A level courses. At present, university mathematicians — people in the territory marked in black in figure 6 — have the greatest influence on A level mathematics syllabuses. But as you can see, A level students then go into medium grey territory and sometimes into the light grey. The medium grey part of higher education has had some influence upon mathematics A level courses, but in a peculiar way. The most popular kind of mathematics A level is the so-called 'pure and applied' syllabus. Oddly, the engineers and scientists have brought their weight to bear on the common core of *pure* topics: they have not had an influence on learning about applying mathematics.

The same arguments could be applied to other subjects. The syllabuses are designed by specialists who are often not concerned or knowledgeable about the destinations of the students who will follow them. And when it comes to designing individual syllabuses, it is hard to find anything in the GCE boards' procedures to ensure that those responsible for related subjects that many candidates will eventually take are consulted.

I have not said nearly enough about those people who take A level with an immediate vocation in view — those forming most of the white part of the bars, shown in the figures of school leaver destinations. Let us not forget that the majority of school students (57 per cent in 1983–84) who had some success at A level did not follow a degree course in the first instance. Many of these students took not three, but one or two A levels. The Higginson Report makes many valuable points. But I think that one of the disappointments of the Higginson Report is that it does not say much about the needs of students who may be taking a range of subjects, and may be capable of A level in some but not in others. The assumption in Higginson seems to be that attainment is uniform: that there are some students who are simply able and there are others who are simply not. And I think that this assumption is regrettable. Here is another issue of breadth which badly needs discussion. And it probably needs discussion in the context of a debate about post-GCSE provision which is wider than the terms of reference of the Higginson Committee.

Vocational Needs

Let us consider someone going from A levels into a vocation. Let us take biology A level as an example. Some students taking an A level course in biology do so as a stepping stone to a nursing qualification. It is no less important that the A level is a suitable preparation for that than it is for 'academic' study. So, as with mathematics, the requirements of biology degree courses should not be the prime influence on the content and skills tested in biology A level.

The same could be said of many other subjects. Yet, once again, it is hard to find any element in the GCE boards' procedures to ensure that those responsible for vocational training — such as course and admission tutors for Higher National Diplomas (HND) and so forth — have been consulted on detail during the process of syllabus development.

The Review of Vocational Qualifications — which gave way to the National Council for Vocational Qualifications (NCVQ) — argued for greater recognition of vocational qualifications for entry into higher education. Robert Jackson has added his voice to those who support better access to higher education for those who have non-standard qualifications. He may have more to say about this when he speaks to you tomorrow (see chapter 7 in this volume). One consequence of these trends might be that A level provision would tend in the future — from pressure of market forces — to approach the style of the vocational courses which are substitutable for them for the purposes of entry to higher education.

Breadth and Higginson

As you know, the Higginson report calls for greater breadth at A level and proposes a standard pattern of five leaner, tougher A levels to provide it. As you also know, the reaction from the Secretary of State, Mr. Baker, has been swift, decisive and negative in relation to the 'five subjects' proposal. Mr. Jackson, on the other hand, has been reported as telling the Royal Society that the subject is not in his view settled and that the debate will continue. Again, we can wait to see whether Mr. Jackson has more to tell us about this tomorrow.

Of course, dividing the A level provision into five rather than three does not automatically provide breadth. Without restrictions on choice such combinations as, physics, chemistry and treble maths would arise. Higginson's recommendation is that breadth should be encouraged by *advice* from within the school. I think you have to recognize that advice will have little effect on school students if they know that that advice will not be relevant to the world beyond school. There are some valuable lessons to be learned from the AS level experience here. One of the factors which inhibits young people from taking AS levels is a concern about how individual admissions tutors will view them. At this point I have to pay tribute to Clive Wake's work in persuading departments first of all to entertain AS levels and then to go public about what they will accept. Preaching to school teachers and preaching by school teachers about breadth will have no effect whatever if the users of the certificates continue to think and act otherwise.

I spoke earlier of A levels as well as AS levels having to play their part in providing breadth. As I say, the main Higginson recommendation does not appear to have government support. But there are other recommendations that have not been publicly overturned and which, in addition to AS levels, do offer scope for breadth as part of reform of A level provision. Higginson talks about the need for general and subject specific principles to govern A level syllabuses, and then a process of revision of syllabuses to bring them into line with these 'principles'. Judging from what Higginson says about these 'principles', I take these to be statements somewhat akin to the general and subject specific criteria of the GCSE. Higginson also sees a need to deal with the proliferation of syllabuses which has occurred. The SEC has not yet commented formally on Higginson, nor is it clear what processes of reform the government would be willing to support. It seems certain that any work to be done will not be done by SEC but by its successor, SEAC, and this body's collective thinking is as yet unknown. But in spite of these uncertainties, those of you who think something needs to be done about A level should not give up hope yet.

Chapter 4

Approaches in some Schools and Colleges

P. Watkins

Introduction

Let me start off by nailing my colours to the mast. I have been committed to the broadening of the sixth form curriculum for over thirty years. When I first went to teach at a grammar school in East London I found that the A level historians that I was teaching were doing four A levels — history, economic history, economics and British Constitution and they wanted to know very little about anything else. I was interested in the early 1960s in the voluntary efforts that were made to broaden the sixth form curriculum, for example, through the General Studies Association and the Agreement to Broaden the Curriculum. (How many people, I wonder, remember that! 360 heads of schools undertook to spend not more than two-thirds of their sixth form time on specialist work and to postpone all specialization to the age of 16. It was like having a nuclear test ban treaty without inspection of each other's arsenals! It didn't last very long). But those were the idealistic sixties. Then from the late sixties there were attempts to reform the system: majors and minors (1966), Q and F (1969) and N and F (1976–79) — what somebody has described as the 'burnt out wagons and discarded trucks of sixth form curriculum reform'.

The narrowness of the sixth form curriculum has in my view been a scandal and continues to be so, even though there is research showing that mixed A levels are now taken by 30 per cent as distinct from 10 per cent of candidates in 1963. It still means that two-thirds of our A level candidates are taking subjects chosen from one side of the arts/science divide. Nor do I believe that general studies is an effective route to broadening the curriculum. I don't doubt that there are schools and colleges that operate very effective systems. My own experience in a number of schools and colleges is that general studies are not taken seriously by staff or students, that they often consist of a series of mini-specialisms and that there is rarely a coherent design to the programme. The most successful courses are recreational, practical and artistic.

The National Scene

Let me now describe the present position of AS in schools and colleges. First a few facts about the national picture drawn from the recent DES survey. AS started in September 1987 with a number of disadvantages. There were no trials, teachers were initially sceptical and there were substantial reservations expressed by all concerned. There was a mismatch between the need and the design. The design was rigour and depth, the need was breadth and relevance. What has actually happened in the first year? Take up in institutions during the first year has been as follows:

— 3 per cent of pupils (6000)
— 15 per cent of institutions (400)
— more sixth form colleges (65 per cent), grammar schools and independent schools than 11–18 comprehensive schools
— most students who are taking AS are taking one subject
— most schools and colleges are offering two or three subjects at AS level.

The most popular subjects, ranked according to student enrolment, have been:

1. general studies
2. mathematics
3. computer studies

The most popular subjects, ranked according to the number of institutions putting on an AS course, have been:

1. mathematics
2. French
3. computing
4. English

Two general points are worth making: in the year of its introduction the gender balance for AS levels is better than for A levels. More boys are taking French, for example, and more girls science and mathematics than would be true of a comparable sample of A level subjects. Second, plans for a 1988 start, collected it is true in January, suggest that there may be a very substantial increase in the number of participants. The Higginson Report may hasten this. The government's target is for 95 per cent of schools to be offering two or more AS level subjects by 1990.

How are Schools Using AS?

Let me turn to what I have gleaned, albeit sometimes anecdotal evidence, from conversations with Heads and other staff, particularly from a number of sixth form colleges but also from 11–18 comprehensive schools. I have the impression that AS as a curriculum component is being used in five different ways.

First, it is being used to provide enrichment and balance for the ablest. Those who are doing three A level subjects are sometimes doing, in addition, one or two AS's. King George V College, Southport, a highly selective sixth form college, says in its brochure that three A plus one AS is 'a heavy load, not to be taken by the faint-hearted'. This is for the ablest an excellent recipe: for those who are studying A level mathematics, physics and chemistry to be also doing French or history AS is highly desirable, just as it is for those who are doing English, history and economics to be adding mathematics or French as an AS, but it is a very tough programme.

Second, and perhaps rather more usually, two A levels plus two AS's is being used as an alternative to three A levels. This is an important growth area because it is a way of increasing the number of subjects normally taken from three to four. It will not of course necessarily ensure breadth but every time you add one more subject you increase the likelihood of breadth. Of the students taking AS at College D, for example (see the case studies later in this chapter), just over half are doing it in this way, two A plus two AS.

Third, an additional subject for the two A level candidate. When I was Principal of a sixth form college, I had pangs of conscience about the candidate who started on two A levels, even though he or she normally added one or two O levels in the first year. When the O level finished it was hard to find a suitable addition to the student's programme and they were sometimes left with two A levels and little else. I was even more exercised by students who started three A levels but by the second year had dropped to two.

Their timetables were very thin indeed — scarcely enough to justify the description of a full time course. And yet it was very difficult to devise courses that they could drop into whenever they had dropped out elsewhere. So a model that starts with two. A plus one AS is at least some improvement and I suspect that it is the second most popular of the five ways in which AS's are being implemented. It is also possible to say to students 'start off on three A levels; you can always drop to two and a half, you don't have to drop to two'.

Fourth, an entirely new constituent for the marginal A level student. This is the student for whom it is scarcely worthwhile embarking on a course of one A level. It becomes more worthwhile embarking on one A plus two AS. College A (see case studies), is an innovative college committed to broadening the curriculum and to meeting the needs of students of lower academic pretensions. It is using one A plus two AS as a way of satisfying the pre-entry requirements of a BEd or CNAA qualification.

And then fifth, there is AS as the main constituent of the sixth form curriculum. Again College A provides an example. There is one student there who is doing four AS's and another who's doing six! You would have seen in the *Times Education Supplement* last week that Liverpool University is going to accept five AS levels as a qualification for reading science. If higher education were to go down this route we might find in due course that AS became the main constituent of the curriculum of some sixth form pupils.

The Case Against Adopting AS

Before I turn to case studies which give examples of the five uses let me turn to the case against adopting AS which I have encountered in talking to schools and colleges. There are five arguments that I have come across.

First there is the preference for the non-examination route to broadening the curriculum. Some schools and colleges have a real commitment to unexamined general studies (or indeed to the general studies A level). Queen Mary College, Basingstoke is well known for its 'main studies'. Ever since the college opened nearly twenty years ago it has devoted a relatively smaller proportion of time to each A level subject than other colleges. The programme has been based on the assumption that main studies were the broad curriculum of which examination courses, particularly at A level, were a part. Queen Mary College has not introduced AS because it does not wish to jeopardize that principle by extending the examined area. Manchester Grammar School at the academic end of the spectrum has well developed programmes of non-examined minority time which it does not wish to compromise by introducing AS.

Where minority time, complementary studies, core studies, general studies or whatever they may be called, are well established there has been opposition to introducing AS. It is not a view I share; it does not, I am afraid, conform to my somewhat cynical opinion of general studies, but it is an outlook I respect.

Second, there are those who have doubts about the acceptability of AS. The universities will not, say the cynics, be interested in candidates with AS as long as they can fill their places with good three A level candidates. It is, say these heads of schools and colleges, the chiefs not the indians in the universities who are in favour of AS. What will admissions tutors actually do when they are faced with a student with three Bs at A level and another with two Bs at A level and two Cs at AS? Will they actually prefer the candidate with two Bs and two Cs because either the student was enlightened enough to tackle four subjects or the school was enlightened enough to insist that he or she did so? That, it seems to me, is a nub question. I hope that those of you in universities and polytechnics will be in a position in 1989 to discriminate positively in favour of those who have chosen to study AS. Doubts about acceptability are very important. The attitude that higher education takes in 1989 will be of the utmost importance in influencing schools, parents and students alike.

The third case against adopting AS is that it will be too demanding. Because of its A level parentage, it is argued by some, it will attract the weaker A level candidate. On the other hand there is, I think, still concern that half an A level equals more than half in time and commitment, particularly if subjects are chosen which do not complement one another. This is a real problem and I hope it will be addressed in due course in the design of syllabuses. If the problem is addressed then it is less obvious that well designed AS levels will be too demanding for students of average ability. One sixth form college in Hampshire said to me that French without prose translation was proving popular and was a way a foreign language might find its way into the sixth form programme of more students, particularly those reading science.

Fourth, we cannot staff it. It is very important that we move to a model, perhaps by using modules, which enables A and AS courses to be taught together, otherwise there is little chance that AS levels will be practicable in comprehensive school sixth forms.

The last reason I was given was innovation fatigue!.

Case Studies

The case studies illustrate the ways in which schools and colleges are introducing AS levels into their course offerings. They also give some indication of the subject provision during the first year that AS levels have been taught, as well as the number of students taking them.

College A

A city sixth form college, 500 students, strong commitment to open access and largest spread of A level subjects in any sixth form college (forty-five in 1982).

1. The college supported AS from the beginning
2. All AS courses last two years
3. Students consider that AS is easier than A level
4. Two target groups:
    — less academic students; 1A + 2AS — as a qualification for BEd or CNAA degree.
    — very able students; 3A + 1 or 2AS (eg French).
5. One student is taking four AS and another six AS subjects.
6. Subject provision:

Inside A level sets		Separate sets	
Subject	Number of students	Subject	Number of Students
World history	3	English	8
Physics	3	French	5
Art	3	Economics	7
		Geography	2
		Computer studies	7
		*Mathematics	6
		Chemistry	5
		Biology	2

*plus students who drop A level Mathematics

7. There are 40 students in all taking eleven AS subjects, with fifty-one examination entries.

School B

A school in rural Dorset catering for 13–18 year olds; 153 in the sixth form; fifty-five A level lower sixth; forty-eight A level upper sixth; forty-five CPVE; fifteen RSA.

1. The school is not keen on the model (i.e. AS equivalent to half A level) and hoped for genuinely developmental syllabuses.
2. There was rigorous counselling of students and none have dropped out of courses.
3. The school encourages 2A + 2AS or 1A + 2AS
4. Students' reaction has been good: they have found the courses stimulating and useful.
5. Subjects offered:

Subject	Examination Board	Number of Students	Notes
Statistics	SEG	10	Biologist and geologists
Theatre studies	London	5	Strong tradition to CSE but no A level
Religious studies	Cambridge	3	Never got an A level set going
Design Technology	Cambridge	5	Started technology as an O level two years ago

College C

An urban sixth form college with 740 students with tradition of independent learning.

1. All courses last two years
2. All courses are separately taught
3. Eight subjects — hoping to offer ten to twelve in September 1988
4. Two sorts of subjects: mathematics, French, English with high demand; music and geology because of low A level take-up
5. Some evidence that students have enjoyed the broadening
6. Has made some inroads into minority time
7. Pupil take-up:
   Forty-four   2A + 1AS
   Five   2A + 2AS
8. Subject provision:

Subject	Boys	Girls
Mathematics	8	2
English	2	5
Biology	1	5
French	1	9
Geology	5	4
Computing	6	4
Music	1	1

College D

A sixth form college located in the South-east.

1. Number of AS levels:

Number	Boys	Girls	Total
1	30	33	63
2	29	24	53
3	1	0	1
	60	57	117

2. Combinations:

	1AS	2AS	Total
With 1A	1	5	6
With 2 or more A's	51	49	100
With other combinations	11	0	11

Usual pattern is 2 or 3A + 1AS
            2 or 3A + 2AS

3. Complementary or contrasting: contrasting AS subjects are regarded by students as harder and less congenial. Complementary AS subjects which support other studies are thought to be easier and are more popular.

College E

Large sixth form college in the South with over 1000 students; 900 taking A level.

1. The College intended to offer five subjects — mathematics, French, English, economics and computer studies. Eventually were unable to staff economics and needed an extra computer studies set at A level
2. Subject take up as follows:

Subject	Boys	Girls	Timetable provision
English	6	13	2½ hours
Mathematics set 1	6	2	2½ hours
Mathematics set 2	8	4	2½ hours
French	4	4	Taught with A level

3. Thirty-eight different students. Most frequent patterns are:
    2A + 1AS
    1A + 1AS + GCSE
    3A + 1AS (very few)
4. The college hopes to offer twelve subjects next year; most will be taught separately but music and home economics to be taught with A level
5. Staff are cautious in advising students to take AS. The safest advice is to take AS as an alternative to a third A level.

College F

Sixth form college in Lancashire with 500 students, all on A level courses.

1. Two year course for 2½ hours per week
2. Typical subject combinations recommended in college brochure are as follows:

A Level	AS Level
physics, chemistry	mathematics, human and social
French, German	biology
geography, geology,	history, industrial studies
chemistry,	human and social biology
geography, economics	mathematics, law
politics, English	industrial studies
art, history	music, English
biology, geography	law
economics, history	religious studies, English

| geography, history | mathematics |
| mathematics, chemistry, biology | law |

3. First year A level students 1987: Sixty students out of 301 (20 per cent) are taking seventy-eight AS subjects.

A level subjects	AS subjects	Number of students	Average Number of O levels
4		16	
3	1	17	8.7
3		193	
2	2	18	7.1
2	1	25	5.7
2		32	

Conclusion

Let me conclude with one or two comments. The route to radical sixth form reform which we followed in the sixties and seventies proved to be a dead end. If the sixth form curriculum is to change in the 1980s it will be by evolution not revolution. I want to suggest that AS can be the starting point for an evolutionary change. There are already signs in the case studies I have shown you of this happening. We must, I believe, encourage the development of contrasting AS levels. They may be harder to sell to students who prefer complementary subjects, which are easier and more congenial. But we ought to encourage contrasting AS levels even if they are harder and less congenial. And by contrast, I mean in style and assessment techniques as well as subject matter. I hope we shall not intepret the AS model as being as restrictive as perhaps it was originally meant to be. We can use AS to broaden the curriculum by a little stretching round the margins. I hope in due course we might zone the curriculum. There might be three or four zones with subjects listed as belonging to one or two zones. Higher education and employers would need to insist that students choose their subjects from at least two zones. That would be a compromise between the prescriptiveness of the International Baccalaureate type of curriculum and the free for all which has produced the highly specialized curriculum of the present day. It will enable university selectors to require greater breadth without being too prescriptive.

I hope we shall encourage innovatory syllabuses at AS. Some

are already in existence, for example, science in society and syllabuses in modern languages and mathematics. There is one called *business in society* that is used at Stoke-on-Trent sixth form college as a pilot A level under the Oxford and Cambridge joint board in association with TVEI: this would make an excellent AS. Lastly, we shall have to sell to students. In the last resort heads and their staff have responsibility for school and college curriculum policy. We shall need to know far more about each other's subjects. We shall develop our counselling skills. I don't think we can go on allowing the sixth form curriculum to be a free for all in which students choose three subjects arbitrarily.

My message is that what is happening is more encouraging than I believed it would be; I shared the reservations everybody else had when AS was announced. I now think that AS can be a route to the development of breadth in the sixth form curriculum, a breadth which is desperately needed if we are to produce an acceptable curriculum for the last years of the century.

Discussion on chapters 3 and 4

Mr. Davidson Mr. Scruton has made a case, not so much for AS levels but for something much more prescriptive, something along the lines of Higginson.

Mr. Scruton I am essentially a libertarian, so I had not intended to make a case for prescription, even if you may think there is one there. I think there is certainly a case for persuasion and I think the universities and polytechnics have to be partners in getting some sort of agreement that breadth is desirable. And I think the universities and polytechnics have then got to go on and say that they actually prefer people who have got this sort of breadth. Currently I think the general attitude to AS levels is that nobody will be preferred if they have AS rather than A levels; in the interim we are aiming for a situation where somebody who has got two A and two AS passes has the same sort of chance as somebody with three similar A level passes. However, I think there are many people who would hope that once we have reached the stage where sixth form and other institutions can provide a reasonable range of AS levels, there might be a case for saying let us have some positive discrimination in favour of those who have got a balanced portfolio of qualifications when they move into higher education.

Conference member You made a brief reference to the content of AS levels. Surely, notwithstanding the skill of those responsible for devising syllabuses and for ensuring that an AS is equivalent to just one half of an A level, students who substitute AS subjects for A levels will always carry a greater burden simply because they are studying more subjects?

Mr. Scruton We have tried to do something positive about that particular point since it is a valid one. The point is that if a student takes a number of subjects from different discipline areas, that student has got to do extra work in order to take on board the ethos of each of these disciplines. It is rather different for someone who is doing say physics, maths and chemistry where one ethos is clearly supporting the next. We recognize that this is something we need to be alert to and accordingly we mention it in our guide lines to the committees that are responsible for approving AS level syllabuses. Now whether the demands made on students are excessive, it is a little bit difficult to judge because you cannot judge the standards in an examination until it has been sat. You cannot just look at the papers and say they are hard; you need to know how to mark, and how demanding the mark schemes are. You also need to know what sort of thresholds there are for the grade boundaries. But your point is definitely taken.

Mr. Burke The Higginson report indicates that room should be made to provide courses with greater flexibility to recognize the varying needs of the whole 16–19 population. Under what criteria would the SEC approve such syllabuses of a more wide ranging nature? The way forward is not to chop the existing A level syllabuses in half. Local authorities will be looking for titles which reflect cross curriculum themes such as economic awareness and communications. How will the SEC view such developments?

Mr. Scruton I think there are probably two or three questions there. If we talk about present SEC practice, there is no problem about setting up a panel for a subject that is of the novel kind. Of course, it is unlikely that the SEC will be approving the next round of A levels; it is almost certain that SEAC will have to do that work and it may have very different procedures. On the question of syllabus breadth there is a tension between meeting the needs of the particular candidate and, indeed, the skills and aptitudes of a particular teacher. However, it is essential not to confuse the user about content. We have to accept the fact that a certificate is a kind of currency, and like a currency its users need to know its value and its worth.

As you will know, with GCSE there has been some cutting down on the title provision, and I think it is generally accepted that that was desirable. But I think there is a case for cutting down still further, there are titles in the GCSE which are frankly risible, *personal services* is one. I do not believe this can go on much longer and in the GCSE it is being looked at. The problem is nothing like so bad at A level because the certificate has actually got to mean something to somebody who is going to employ a student or take him into a polytechnic or university. Now that does not mean that we shall not, perhaps, be aiming for a situation in which we have standard titles which have standard criteria, or principles, to use the Higginson word, which nevertheless allow the teacher to put a particular emphasis on a subject because of the needs of the student, the organization of the institution, or the skills of the teacher himself. We already have something a bit like that at GCSE with the science criteria, which are umbrella criteria, applying to all sciences. With reference to these criteria the aim is to set down clearly the sorts of skills required in each subject, and make some statements about the integrity of the content of the syllabus. It may be that this is one way forward in dealing with A levels. However, on this point I must stress that the SEC has not discussed this yet, and when it does discuss it the view that it takes may well be different from my own.

Mrs. Wall Do you think there is any prospect for the development of modular A and AS levels on an extensive basis? If such a development did occur it might then be possible to select modules from different subjects in order to broaden the range of subjects studied by the back door. A single grade might be obtained for a combination of modules drawn from two subjects. Would this be encouraged?

Mr. Scruton We do, of course, have a session on this tomorrow, but as far as SEC is concerned when modular syllabuses come to us for comment we do insist that if somebody can get a certificate by winging their way through some modules, then the possible route has got to be defined, and the certificate which is given at the end has got to be distinct and clearly descriptive of what has gone on.

Conference member How far have we looked at the experiences of the continental countries and of Scotland to see how their educational systems satisfy their needs.

Mr. Watkins The question of how one should set about curriculum development is an important one. We have tried a number of different ways, but in fact there has never really been a curriculum development policy. The questioner is quite right in implying that had there been such a policy then the Scottish model might well have been one that we would have looked at very much more carefully.

Professor Wake On the university side, or at any rate at SCUE, we are very interested in the Scottish experience. We admire it a great deal, as we do also the International Baccalaureate. What is rather paradoxical about the present situation is that more and more universities are admitting more and more IB students and one would expect that this would flow — and I hope that it will flow over — into a broadening of the A level system.

Mr. Ely I was very interested in Mr. Watkins' five ways of using AS levels, but I am concerned about the fourth, that is the entirely new constituent formed largely of marginal A level students. If the material covered in AS turns out to be, as intended, every bit as difficult as A levels, and if the fears that have already been voiced that doing two AS subjects involves more time than just one A level, then the question that immediately arises is: is it sensible to put this sort of pupil in for one A plus two AS levels as opposed to two A levels? It is by no means certain that the option that includes AS levels is easier for the marginal student.

Mr. Watkins It is not necessarily easier, it could be better. I do not believe that the original aim of half an A level is practicable nor do I believe it will happen. In due course syllabuses will be designed in a different way so that they do not represent an A level chopped in half. If you assume an A level in history consists of two essay papers of three hours each and AS consists of one then you have achieved nothing. It will be important to design AS from scratch then you could come up with syllabuses that are more appropriate for the candidates taking them without deviating too markedly from the design.

Mr. Brown I am responsible for administration in a tertiary college and it seems to me that you (Mr. Watkins) have been somewhat selective in the examples that you have used.

Mr. Watkins No, I have no ulterior motive. I contacted people I knew. I realize that the sample is unduly representative of sixth form colleges because they are using AS a great deal and because I know many principals. I know much less about what is going on in tertiary colleges. At the moment you need to be a big institution committed to curriculum development to have started AS last September. If this conference is held again in twelve months time, we shall have a more balanced sample to draw on and be able to select examples from comprehensive schools, grammar schools, sixth form colleges and tertiary colleges.

Conference member I am concerned about the very term broadening. All references to broadening implicitly assume that it is the existing curriculum that needs to be broadened. But surely as we move towards the next century we ought to be concentrating on alternative sources of students for the higher education sector — alternative that is to those coming up through the traditional route.

Mr. Watkins Various vocational routes into higher education are currently open to candidates. For example, in the latest edition of *University Entrance*, BTEC qualifications are prominently mentioned. Although AS is not particularly relevant to this particular clientele, other things certainly are.

Mrs. Bell I teach in a school with a relatively small sixth form and I don't think that we are going to be able to provide the resources for separate AS level courses. Up until today I had assumed that AS and A level students would be taught in the same group. Now I am not so sure that this is going to be possible.

Mr. Watkins I recognize that it will be very important for schools to be able to timetable A and AS level sets together if they are to offer AS at all. In some subjects this would be easier than others. For example, in history it is relatively easy, less so in the sciences. Do look at the Swindon example where they appear to have succeeded by using a modular structure. You will also need to shop around for syllabuses in order to find those which can most readily be taught alongside A level courses. There should in due course be examples of successful practice and perhaps local authority 16–19 advisers might make a point of collecting them.

Mr. Scruton I think Peter and I share common ground in feeling that it is those AS levels which are designed from scratch which are going to provide the real educational benefit for the future. I think that is the message that you should have picked up from both of us, but the fact remains that if you do want to shop around for something which is half an A level, there are an awful lot of syllabuses of that kind available from the examining boards. I think there probably are some pedagogical problems about co-teaching these sets. These problems are related to differential rates of progress of the two sets. For example, take mathematics and physics, where very often the AS level is closely tied to the core. If both sets are taught together this means one group can take two years to acquire the basic core while the other group will need to assimilate the core — or most of it — over a shorter period in order to be able to spend the rest of the two year period applying it. There is something funny about this sort of mis-match that arises from co-teaching. However, there are certainly a lot of syllabuses that one can shop around and choose from.

Mr. Little I am getting a little confused with all this. We have been told that we have to maintain the standard of A levels while at the same time we have been told about those universities which will admit our students to do chemistry degrees when they only have AS level chemistry. We have been told about Liverpool taking students with five AS levels instead of three A levels and we have heard about 'designed from scratch' AS levels and alternative routes into higher education. It is beginning to sound a bit like Higginson in disguise.

Section III
The Examination Boards

Chapter 5

Syllabus Developments

Simon Loveday

I ought to make it clear at the outset that I am a Subject Officer; I am not a Research Officer. However at the examination boards the dividing line between Research Officer and Subject Officer is not a clear one because if you are running a subject you are involved in the research needed for syllabus development, and if you are a Research Officer then inevitably you are researching into subjects. So, there is a considerable overlap between the two jobs. That said the area that I have been working intensively in for the last few years is syllabus development.

Choices to be Made

When drawing up an AS syllabus, or any other syllabus come to that, there are a lot of conflicting demands to be met. Table 1 shows some of the choices that have to be made in syllabus development as a result of forces that pull in opposite directions.

Should the syllabus be free standing or co-teachable? Will it have a pattern of options or will it have a very fixed structure? Will it be very new, or will it be very familiar? And, to put it very crudely, will it be easy or hard? These may be fairly homely terms, and it may sound a bit embarrassing to say, 'We would like an AS that is ever so easy so that people can get good grades at it', but I think somebody needs to say it all the same, because if you are encouraging your students to go in for this new kind of examination you want to be sure that they get a fair reward for their work at the end of it.

Table 1:   *Choices to be made in syllabus development*

Free-standing	or	Co-teachable
Options	or	Fixed choice
Familiar	or	New
Easy	or	Hard

Free-standing or Co-teachable?

Now, let us look at these choices, and these forces, in a little more detail. The first choice that has to be made is whether you want a free-standing or a co-teachable AS — that is one that is nothing to do with the corresponding A level, or a co-teachable one that has a very strong overlap with the A level, and is, perhaps, a subset of it. The advantage of a free-standing AS is that you can use it as a vehicle for syllabus development. It has a distinct identity, students who go in for it know that it is something special. It can cater for a separate population, and that is intellectually exciting. The major problem with a course that is free-standing is that of timetabling; organizing all your AS teaching separately from your A level teaching in a given subject must raise considerable complications. And of course there are also staffing difficulties, particularly in small schools and colleges. As for standard, we are supposed to be linking AS levels to A level. The initial brief from the DES was that AS should be of A level standard but achievable in half the teaching time. Now we have heard very different views as to what that A level linkage should be, but nonetheless there must be some, I think. A danger in making the new AS level courses completely free-standing would be the potential loss of A level linkage that might result.

Options or fixed choice?

The second choice that has to be made concerns options. Are you going to go for a very varied pattern of options? If you offer lots of options, you will produce a very flexible course that will cater for a wide range of students. Take, for example, a subject like French. You may feel that you want a French course that will appeal to the physicist, the chemist, the historian and the student of English, as well as the linguist. You may want a business studies option, and so on. And obviously, a pattern of options of this kind is very attractive to students. However, as Dr. Kingdon hinted this morning, the boards have to balance their budgets. An AS with a very flexible pattern of options can be very complex and very expensive. It can be an administrative nightmare for the board and, of course, there are problems of comparability between the various patterns of options. Now these are in many ways research matters, and all the boards face these problems. There are no easy answers, but one does have to be aware of them. I think that is the theme I am going to keep coming back to. There are plenty of questions, but a distinct shortage of answers.

New or familiar?

Should the new syllabuses break new ground, be progressive and exciting, or should there be no attempt to innovate, but rather an emphasis on what is familiar? Students themselves are not terribly innovative and their parents tend to prefer what is familiar rather than new — at least in matters concerning their children's education. And we should not forget what has already been referred to as teacher exhaustion. Everybody — teachers, students and parents — has had quite a lot of new developments to adjust to in recent years and this itself would suggest that we ought, perhaps, to be cautious in our pursuit of progressivity.

Easy or hard?

On the question of how easy or how hard the new AS syllabuses should be, common sense would seem to dictate that a balance needs to be struck. If they are made too easy they will lack credibility. If they are made too hard they will end up with few students taking them. Thus, something half way between O and A level might seem about right; but half way in what sense? In depth, or in breadth, or in both?

The requirement that AS levels should be of A level standard, but achievable in half of the time suggests that they will — if they are not already — be regarded as half of an A level. To equate AS with half an A level is a crude generalization, but what does it mean? We can only attempt an answer to this by reference to the depth and breadth (i.e., range) of the syllabus.

Half an A Level

In order to pursue this further let us suppose that the box in figure 1 is what an A level has within it. It has a certain depth of difficulty and a certain breadth, or range of coverage. The question then is: 'How are we going to turn this into an AS level?' The answer may, of course, differ from one subject to another.

The contents of the box can be halved by cutting the box in two, either horizontally or vertically. Figure 2 shows the horizontal cut. Clearly a horizontal cut implies a reduction in depth which is unacceptable if the AS course is supposed to be of A level difficulty

Figure 1   Half an A level?

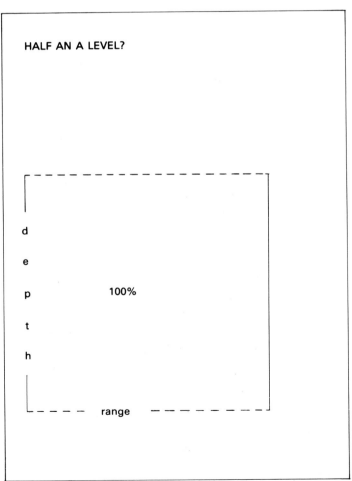

HALF AN A LEVEL?

d

e

p   100%

t

h

range

Figure 2   The horizontal cut

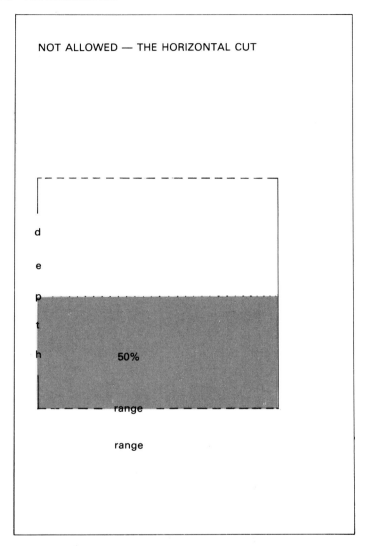

but half the subject content and achievable in half the time. The horizontal cut gives rise to a kind of AO solution where *everything* is done to a reduced level of sophistication and difficulty. Some might regret this. One of the points that has been made from the audience today is that AS could have offered the opportunity to increase the sixth form population, to increase the range of people who could take further examinations. But built into AS is this requirement of A level difficulty and rigour. The brief the boards were given was to make it of A level difficulty, but with half the teaching time and half the content. Therefore, the horizontal cut is ruled out.

The second option is the vertical cut (see figure 3 below). Here depth is retained but there is a loss of coverage. This is a solution that has been quite widely adopted and it certainly looks very

Figure 3 The vertical cut

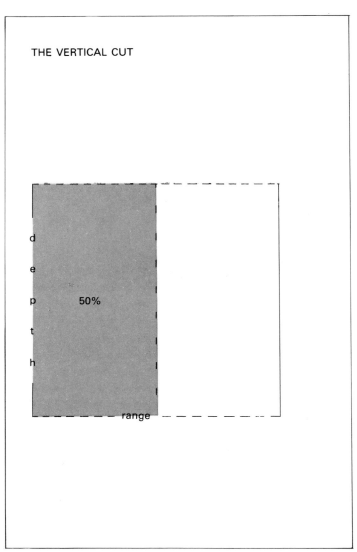

simple and appealing. I believe that in fact it is not quite as simple and easy as it looks, but I am going to leave it to Dr. Kingdon to explain exactly why this is so.

One problem that arises when subjects are split down the middle is what has been called the unitary subject problem. A unitary subject is one which is so integrated, so much all of a piece, that it cannot be divided. In fact I have yet to come across anybody in any subject area who actually admits that his subject can be divided down the middle; this is something that most of us believe is only possible for other peoples' subjects, not our own. In short, most of us believe that our own subject is a unitary subject.

Unitary Subjects

As an example of the unitary subject problem let us look at the case of modern languages. Any modern language can be said to consist of four skills: speaking, listening, reading and writing. If we are devising a new syllabus, which of these skills do we concentrate on? In terms of the figures referred to we could make a vertical cut and have a kind of speaking and listening AS, but that would give rise to a few problems (see figure 4 below). Although there is not a lot of time I should like to tell you quickly how my own board — the Oxford Delegacy — tackled this problem.

When the decision to go ahead with AS levels was actually made in 1985 we wrote to all our centres and asked them which subjects they thought were most interesting and relevant. It was clear from the responses that we had that modern languages were very popular, and we were not surprised by this. We had a very good response from the schools and we got about twenty-five teachers together in the autumn of 1985. We asked them: 'What kind of AS levels in modern languages do you want?' We spent the morning looking at the various existing post-16 schemes — the Leeds AO scheme, the WoW scheme, the FLIC scheme and the FLAW scheme.[1] In the afternoon we split the teachers up into smaller groups and asked each to report back with its recommendations. And when they came back, three of the four groups said, 'We want an AS without any writing in the foreign language — but of course the universities will never accept it'. And the fourth group, although it came up with something different, indicated that it too would have liked to recommend the 'no writing' approach but had not done so on the grounds that it

Figure 4   The 'unitary subject' problem: the case of modern languages

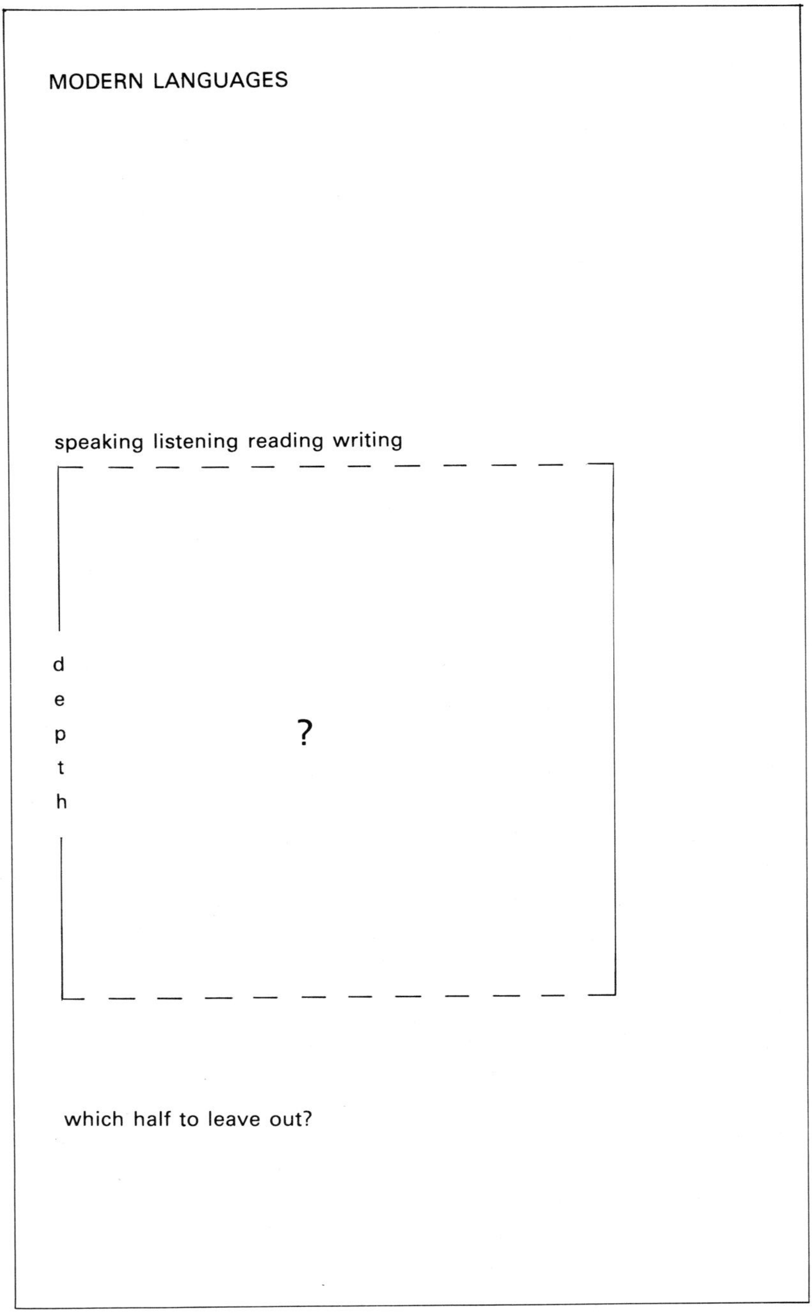

MODERN LANGUAGES

speaking listening reading writing

d
e
p
t
h

?

which half to leave out?

believed the universities would never accept such a qualification. For our part we were persuaded that this was a reasonable way of proceeding, that the risk was worth taking, and we set about persuading the universities that this was so.

Our particular response to AS in modern languages illustrates that although small boards might not have all the ideas, they can nevertheless take more chances. Of course, the climate of opinion has changed; we thought it was amazingly brave in 1985 to go for an AS level in modern languages in which no writing in the foreign language was required. But we were soon to realize that we were not as *avant garde* as we had thought ourselves to be. In the spring of 1986 there was a big language conference at JCLA and we went along to talk about how we were planning to launch our AS levels. Of the five boards represented at the conference, three announced quite independently that they too were going to try for an AS without any writing in the foreign language. So that is how Oxford's AS in modern languages was set up. It is going to have some speaking, but not quite such a long oral as A level; it will have some listening, but we leave out some of the A level material; likewise, reading will be included but not all that is covered at A level; writing in the foreign language will not be examined. Although we would not claim that this is perfect, or indeed the only, answer, it is one way forward. It is one way of moving from a 100 per cent A level syllabus to only 50 per cent of that syllabus without, we think, sacrificing standards. What we end up with is an AS that consists almost entirely of elements from the A level.

One last point I want to make to you, and I want to connect it to the handout which you have in front of you. You will see from it that almost all the delegacy's AS's are co-teachable. This is a decision which the delegates, our governing body, took in 1985, and I think it is probably unique in being the only decision taken by the governing body which staff actually agreed with! What I particularly want to say here is that there is not a hard line between, on the one hand, stale old stuffy co-teachable AS's, which are just like the boring old A levels you know all about, and on the other hand, innovative, exciting, all-singing, all-dancing non-co-teachable AS levels which are part of a new development. If I may return to modern languages, this point comes across rather clearly. When we were devising our modern languages AS for 1989, with the brief to make it co-teachable, we had a huge new syllabus revision already planned for 1990. So the question was, how could we make our 1989 co-teachable AS syllabus co-teachable with an A level syllabus that did not yet exist? Clearly there were problems to sort out here but basically what we decided was to use our AS syllabus development as part of the overall process of review and development, to learn the lessons from that development, and to build them into the A level for 1990. So what I would like to leave you with is the point that there does not have to be an opposition between the old and familiar and the new and different, but it is sometimes possible to marry the two in a constant process of revision. AS can be a part of that process, and what you can end up with is something which is not only a new AS but also a new A level.

Note

1   World of Work (WoW), Foreign Languages in the Community (FLIC), Foreign Languages at Work (FLAW).

Chapter 6

Some Practical Issues for Chief Examiners

M. Kingdon

AS level examinations have presented the examining boards with new problems of a technical nature. These result from the initial proposals for the examination which contained the somewhat simplistic belief that common A and AS level components would be a means to ensuring comparability of grading between the two levels. It is this issue that I principally wish to address. I also intend to consider some of the practical issues that will face the AS level chief examiners in 1989. I will pose the fundamental question about the new examination: 'What, in terms of academic standards, will half an A level actually mean?' To answer this issue I propose to consider two subsidiary questions: 'What are the principles underlying A level standards?' and 'How will these principles have to be adapted for AS level awards?'

The Award of A and AS Level Grades

The general approach to the determination of GCE A level grades has been a qualitative assessment of performance supported by quantitative checks. These processes have usually involved the consideration of four forms of comparability:

(a) *Comparability between years*
This form of comparability is perhaps the most important but it will not be a meaningful issue when each AS level syllabus is examined for the first time, thereafter it will be.

(b) *Comparability between syllabuses*
This form of comparability has usually been achieved by the shared experience of the chief examiners of the

different syllabuses within the same subject. This is the approach that most Boards are likely to adopt in order to achieve comparable A and AS level awards.

(c) *Comparability between Boards*
     Once again, this will not be an issue in the first year of AS levels but may become one if the new examination develops as expected.

(d) *Comparability between different subjects*
     This form of comparability has usually been investigated using post award statistical procedures — 'subject pairs analysis' — and this principle will probably be carried over into AS level examinations.

The introduction of AS levels will create a fifth form of comparability, namely that between A and AS levels in the same subject.

(e) *Comparability of A and AS level syllabuses in the same subject*
     This form of comparability will probably be assessed both qualitatively and quantitatively using methods (b) and (c) above.

Depth and Breadth

In the early documents relating to the AS level examination it seems to have been assumed that depth and breadth are independent features of attainment. Further, it was assumed that common A and AS level components would assist in ensuring the comparability of awards.

I intend to dismiss the first of these beliefs straight away. It would seem from current inter-GCE Board research that one of the most valued features of A level attainment is the ability of a candidate to range over and to demonstrate control of the content, skills and principles that underpin a subject at 18+. (Some would use the phrase 'mastery' in this context.) Such an ability must depend on breadth. (Using Simon Loveday's models, greater depth seems to require greater breadth to support it.) If we apply this logic the other way round, less breadth of study in a subject will imply less depth. I am therefore making the assumption that even if A and AS level syllabuses have some common components, the AS level candidates will not generally perform as well as their A level colleagues.

Common Components and Comparability

To consider the second assumption, — that common A and AS level components would assist in ensuring the comparability of awards — we need to identify the different relationships between A and AS level syllabuses in the same subjects. Four forms exist:

(i) Freestanding AS level syllabuses which have been developed independently of any previous 17+ or 18+ examinations in the same subject;

(ii) AS level syllabuses derived from former Alternative Ordinary levels;

(iii) A and AS level syllabuses with common questions and sections;

(iv) A and AS level syllabuses with common components. (For the purposes of this talk I am going to define an examination component as any part of an examination that has its own separate mark total.)

The first of my four categories — the freestanding AS level syllabuses will have to be awarded in 1988 solely on the basis of chief examiner opinion. The chief examiner will have to make assessments in the light of what they think it is reasonable for an 18+ candidate, who has studied a subject over two years and for the recommended number of hours, to have achieved.

The same principle will also have to apply to awards of any AS level syllabuses which are based on former AO levels. It is necessary to point out, however, that the standards of AS levels will be higher. If AS levels are to represent about four periods a week, extended over two years (in effect 5+ terms), and if AS levels are to be taken by 18+ candidates, this will represent a significant increment in standard over an examination which was taught for four to six periods a week, over one year (2+ terms) and written with 17-year-olds in mind.

Common questions and sections will not be a useful guide to A and AS level standards unless the opportunities are taken both to analyse the performances of the two groups of candidates on the common elements prior to any award, *and* the likely relationship between A and AS levels is clearly understood. This will not be the case in the first year of the AS level examination. Attempts to understand the relationships between the first AS level syllabuses and associated A levels will have to be a post first award activity. (Even the success of such an exercise is not guaranteed. As

Newbould and Massey (1979) have demonstrated, common elements may not be as great a help in assessing comparabilities even *within a single level* as is generally believed.)

I am not dismissing the possibility that in some subjects A and AS level candidates will perform equally well on common components, sections and questions. What I am saying is that I think it is unlikely and that it is a dangerous assumption to make in 1989.

Conclusion

The conclusion that I draw is that the only basis for the award of AS level grades in 1989 is the chief examiners' assessment of what they expect of candidates: who are 18+; are doing other 18+ examinations; have studied the AS level syllabuses for two years; and, for the recommended time. Assessments of the comparability of one AS with another or an AS level syllabus with an A level in the same subject will be undertaken after the first results are published.

References

NEWBOULD, C.A. and MASSEY, A.J. (1979) *Comparability Using a Common Element*, Test Development and Research Unit, Occasional Publication 7, Cambridge.

Discussion on chapters 5 and 6

Ms. Johnson In Simon Loveday's handout he indicates that only forty per cent of AS physics is a subject of A level physics. I don't understand how, in such a situation, one can co-teach physics.

Mr. Loveday The explanation of the 40 per cent is that this proportion of the questions on the AS examination paper is selected from questions that are set for A level.

Ms. Johnson And the other 60 per cent is not from the A level paper?

Mr. Loveday It is more precise to say that the other sixty per cent consists of different questions; they are not set on different syllabuses.

Conference member Could I follow up on that and ask what the criteria for co-teaching area; and if you inform the schools of these criteria?

Mr. Loveday Co-teaching raises difficult issues and we felt that you really had to have some idea at the start whether that was what you were aiming for. We believed that if we set a broadly common syllabus or an AS syllabus which fell within the boundaries of the A level syllabus then that could be co-teachable. In languages, I tried to explain that the AS syllabus consists almost entirely of elements occurring in the A level. In short the full AS syllabus is a sub-set of the A level syllabus. Thus, there isn't a chunk of the AS syllabus that is AS only, necessitating separate teaching. The questioner asks just what it is that we tell the schools.

Just putting the question raises another, namely 'to what extent, if any, is it the business of the examination boards to tell schools what to do?' One may take the view that it is not our business to tell schools what to teach but simply to set the examinations. I have always felt that this is a somewhat disingenuous position to take since the examinations we set have a very, very, powerful effect on what teachers in schools teach. However, there is, of course, a difference between influencing what is taught and telling schools how to teach their subjects. The boards have no desire to do the latter. Now this co-teachable question depends, I think, on what kind of candidates are coming forward. Although the Oxford Delegacy deals with a smaller number of candidates than, say, the London Board, the evidence that we have does not suggest that bright students only opt for A level, with the less bright opting for AS. In a mixed class some of the AS candidates will be doing it because they are not up to A level and some because they just haven't got the hours to do an A level, even though they are actually very able and are pursuing the AS in one of their best subjects. Now if the population is not divided in such a way that the better students only do A level while the weaker ones all do AS, then we would expect that a co-teachable syllabus would be appropriate. However, there are seven examining boards offering a range of syllabuses and it is up to you to choose the one that best suits your school and your students.

Dr. Kingdon I have got very little to add to what Simon has said. When the first AS proposals appeared in 1984 there was a fear amongst some teachers that AS levels would become something for failed A level candidates. However, in the surveys and case study visits that have been undertaken we have not found this to be the case. We have found the relationships between A and AS as Simon has described them. Certainly there are some students who have started AS courses but later changed to A level and others have moved from A to AS. Our observations are quite reassuring: we have found many students who in the next academic year are actually thinking of upgrading themselves from A to AS because they have found that they like the subject.

Mrs. Price May I follow-up Mr. Loveday's answer on the forty per cent physics paper: do I understand you to mean that there are identical questions and would they therefore be marked at the same level, particularly in view of what was said earlier about expecting different standards?

Mr. Loveday I have a paper which I have just circulated to my colleagues, which is on precisely this matter of how we grade AS relative to A level. That paper is going to be discussed by a working party and therefore we do not have an official view on it at the moment. However, I can tell you my own personal view on this matter. And to be honest it is that we should mark and have marking schemes which are identical but have grading meetings which are different. This is a very complex area and I don't want to say more than that.

Dr. Kingdon In the University of London School Examinations Board we considered this problem and decided very early on that it was going to be unrealistic to expect the same qualitative or quantitative performance from A and AS level candidates on common components. Once again I reiterate that I'm not dismissing the possibility of equal performance but we do not yet know and will not know until after the first examination of each syllabus has taken place whether it is realistic to expect equal performance. There may be some instances where equal performance could occur. When ULSEB designed its syllabuses we tended to avoid, more than other boards, the use of common components. We have some syllabuses which fit into Simon's one hundred per cent category where all of the AS components are to be found within existing A level ones and we have quite a number of instances where the AS level components are in fact the first half of A level papers. Where we have common components the syllabus developers decided that in the 1989 examination the number of AS candidates would not be particularly large so we would try and analyze, between the examination being taken and our briefing for markers, just what the AS level candidates will have done in the examination. At that stage we may well issue a different mark scheme for AS which will seek to reward features of performance differently. But this is all very open at the moment and I'm talking about things that will happen a year from now. We — the Board's officers — will be actively looking at these problems and I think it really requires us — all boards — to issue informative subject and research reports on the 1989 examinations to explain exactly what was found, what was done and what the consequences for A and AS level candidates were.

Mr. Loveday I would just like to make the point that there is a considerable overlap between examiners and teachers. At the Oxford Delegacy the number of examiners who are teachers is very high; the percentage who are academics is very low. So examiners are not a species who are wheeled out once a year to be horrible to candidates; they do know what happens in classrooms.

Mr. Brenchley I would like to ask a fairly technical question which will be of considerable interest, I think, to people working in further education establishments. But I hope those working in schools will also take note of it. The National Council for Vocational Qualifications is approving the competence elements of national vocational qualifications at present. It seems to me, particularly from the list of subjects produced by the Oxford Delegacy, there are a number of subjects which have a considerable amount of common ground with what will in due course be national vocational qualifications. Can you tell me if your boards are at present having any discussions with national vocational examining bodies which might result in AS levels counting towards a national vocational qualification. I am thinking of discussions similar to those taking place between the RSA and the Southern Examining Group over GCSE?

Mr. Loveday I am not sure whether this is an inter-board matter, something to be discussed between the NCVQ and the boards or whether it is a higher level matter involving SEC or SEAC. We certainly are aware of the discussions referred to but I do not know whether the examining boards are engaged in similar discussions.

Dr. Kingdon The only thing that I know is that discussions are taking place at three different levels. Insofar as my own board is concerned, we have received correspondence from the NCVQ and we are talking to them about some syllabuses. I am also aware that the GCE boards collectively, through the Committee of Secretaries, are also discussing this because some things have been passed for comment to the Research Officers. I should imagine that the NCVQ is also talking to the SEC but Paul Scruton would obviously be able to confirm whether or not such talks are taking place.

Mr. Scruton The answer is that although we have an observer of the NCVQ, we do not at present carry out any liaison with them on a subject basis. The idea has been talked about, informally, but to date nothing has been agreed.

Conference member If a candidate fails A level can the marks for the common papers count towards an AS?

Dr. Kingdon I hinted at this this morning in my first presentation when I said that in the Higher School Certificate system you could fail a main course but get a subsidiary pass. That is definitely not going to be allowed in the AS level context. Our rules are that you cannot co-enter an A and an AS level and there certainly will be no possibility of a candidate ending up with an AS level as a consolation prize for failing the A level.

This is definitely not going to be permitted for two reasons: firstly it would encourage the idea of AS level as a fallback position for failed A level candidates, and the boards are against it for this reason: secondly, the SEC will not permit it.

Section IV
Government Policy

Chapter 7

Government Policy on A and AS Levels

Robert Jackson

A conference on the subject of AS levels is timely. I would like to underline the government's very strong commitment to broadening the sixth form curriculum and the key role of AS levels in bringing this about as part of our plans for raising educational standards; to explain our views in more detail now AS courses are up and running and higher education has made progress in adapting course requirements.

Higginson and A Levels

The Higginson report was published on 7 June and it is clear that there are a number of misconceptions in circulation. There have been press reports saying that the government have rejected Higginson: that we knew in advance that we did not want to change the A level system so what was the point in setting up the committee. This is not true. The central thrust of the report is the need for the sixth form curriculum to be broader. The government agrees, which is why it introduced AS levels. Where we disagree is on Higginson's proposal for achieving breadth by streamlining A level syllabuses and reducing time on them, and, as a result, reducing their factual content.

We do not believe that this can be achieved without loss of standards. We should not forget that A levels are a tried and tested system which has guaranteed excellence over many years. Higher education, employers, schools, parents and the young people themselves know that and rightly prize them. A levels provide a sound basis for our three year degree course. I know Higginson did not consider that his proposals would have any knock-on effect in higher education. But we are not convinced that such a radical change to our system, as proposed, would not put these standards at risk. We hear much about the advantages of our competitors but little about the high drop-out rates in the first year of their undergraduate courses.

The committee's remit was in fact to draw up principles to govern syllabuses and their assessment, and this they have done. Fears have been expressed that young people who have become used to the teaching and learning approaches of GCSE will find it difficult to cope with A levels. This is to misunderstand the nature of A levels and of GCSE. A levels are not at a standstill: they are developing all the time. Some well-tried syllabuses already in-corporate an active approach to learning and the report published by HMI last year, *Experiencing A levels — Aspects of Quality*, which was based on inspections carried out in 1984–85, noted that much of the best quality A level teaching seen laid stress on developing oral and practical skills and on the understanding and application of knowledge, and reached very high standards of achievement, both in personal learning and in exam results.

So the ongoing process of developing and revising A level syllabuses will take account of best practice, and will have the Higginson principles to guide them. What the government does not think is necessary or desirable is to engage in an overhaul of all syllabuses now. The system has a substantial programme of reform already and cannot be asked to cope with more change at present. We do not in any case think it necessary.

I would like to pay tribute here to how well and professionally teachers have responded to the first year of GCSE. We expected the first year to be hard work and we appreciate their effort and dedication to GCSE.

AS Levels

Discussion of the sixth form curriculum has been going on for years with little result. There was a clear wish to broaden but no agreement on how. Proposals were made for an intermediate exam but were rejected because the exam did not lead anywhere. Higher education and industry were unenthusiastic. The advantage of AS levels is that, requiring the same standard of work as A levels, although only half the study time, they are locked into the A level system and thus provide a guarantee of quality to higher education and industry in line with known admission standards. They are not something on the side which can be ignored or which can be seen as an easy option. They therefore provide the potential for genuine broadening.

Who wants them? Higher education and industry certainly do as the following quotes show:

> The Committee of Vice-Chancellors and Principals firmly believes in the importance of broadening the sixth form curriculum, and sees the introduction of AS levels as a significant practical step in this direction.
>
> The CNAA welcomes the introduction of AS levels and will accept two AS level passes as the equivalent of an A level pass for entry to courses.
>
> In supporting the introduction of AS levels, the CBI favours the taking of contrasting subjects, since it has consistently advocated the need for broadening the sixth form curriculum, so that students will have a wider career choice open to them.
>
> A modern language course directed at students taking science, for example, would provide a broadening and useful set of skills.... A statistics course aimed at students of the humanities would provide breadth and would contrast with the main areas of study. (*The Higginson Report*, 1988)

These elements are there in AS levels. Young people can choose to take one or more AS levels in addition to, or in place of, one of their intended A levels and thus continue for longer with subjects which they enjoy and which can help to enhance their study and job options later. They can choose to do subjects which complement or contrast with their chosen field of study at A level. Contrasting subjects are particularly to be commended: we need to have more engineers and businessmen who can converse and conduct business with their opposite numbers in other countries.

What is the reality? A slow start? This is not really surprising because we did not impose AS levels and schools and colleges had other things to think about. But the way ahead is now clear and we want to see schools and colleges build AS increasingly into their sixth form provision.

This year over 6500 students started AS courses, most doing

one but 600 attempting two. Nearly 15 per cent of schools and 10 per cent of colleges with A levels are offering some courses. Next year, about half of schools and colleges have said they intend to offer AS courses. In sixth form and tertiary colleges, the figure rises to nearly three quarters. We want to encourage individual institutions and LEAs to look positively at sixth form provision and to do their best to plan for some AS courses.

We do not underestimate the difficulty in some schools, but a fresh look at the disposition of time and resources in general studies and non-examined time could make all the difference. We very much hope that by 1990, most institutions will offer at least two courses.

Where numbers on AS courses are significant, ideally they can be taught separately. This can be an enriching experience for all the students because of the heterogeneity of the group. It may be difficult to introduce AS courses in small sixth forms, and particularly to arrange separate teaching. In those circumstances, it may be possible to introduce some AS provision where students can be taught alongside those on A level courses. A word of warning — higher education told us they set great store by the maturing experience of the two year course. In some circumstances, of course, AS courses will be taken in one year. There would be more concern if AS levels were taken as a preparation or try out for A level. Higher education have said they will not accept the same subject at A and AS level for entry.

Some evidence in year one also shows that AS levels are most successful where they have been introduced into recognizable programmes of examined and non-examined provision, and where students have had guidance to put together a broad and balanced programme. These principles of breadth and balance are no less important post-16. Higginson spoke of the importance of guidance for students in study choices.

And what about students? We know they enjoy AS levels. We are publishing a booklet today which has been sent to all secondary schools and to colleges containing interviews with some of the first takers.

A boy doing three science A levels and French:

> It seemed such a big step — choosing whether to do science or languages. I wanted to do medicine but my parents were keen for me to carry on with a language because I am quite good at them. So AS level was an ideal opportunity.

A girl is taking computer studies and electronics at AS level in addition to A levels in history and English literature:

I think that my A levels will stand me in good stead, while the AS levels will show employers that I'm prepared to do something different.

What worries teachers, parents and students most? Whether higher education will accept AS levels. Will young peoples' chances be prejudiced by taking them? Higher education have said not. All universities, including the medics, accept two AS levels in place of a third A level. Bradford, Durham, East Anglia, Keele, Lancaster and London will accept four AS levels. But the real interest is in the individual course requirement. Will admissions tutors who have had the pick of the A level bunch up to now ignore AS levels? The universities say not. The official guide, *University Entrance*, shows increasing progress: more and more courses will accept AS levels as approved subjects.

I want to pay tribute to the considerable amount of work put into promoting AS levels by CVCP, SCUE and CNAA; we want to see even greater progress in accepting AS levels in place of named A levels. I would urge universities to look carefully at what they require and to be flexible in the offers they make to give full value to AS levels. You are not being asked to lower standards: these young people are the traditional A level cohort. A guided combination of good A and AS levels represents a considerable achievement on the part of a young person, some would say even more so than achieving three A levels.

Schools and parents will be looking hard at how the first applicants fare this autumn. Numbers will be small but how higher education treats them will be crucial to AS levels and important for higher education because it will rightly be seen as a test of commitment to broadening. Higginson noted that a number of young people well capable of A levels did not do them or fell by the wayside because they had chosen the wrong subjects. AS levels can also help some of these by providing more choice and the possibility of putting together a programme more related to their interests.

Some interesting research has been done recently at Salford University which concluded that the physics requirement for most courses of engineering could be contained within an AS level. We need more studies on these lines, and a willingness on the part of academics and examining boards to work together to produce or modify existing AS syllabuses so as to meet these requirements. As the number of 18- to 20-year-olds fall, AS levels will be increasingly important in helping to extend options for study.

A word on syllabuses. Over 100 have been approved, and higher education has scrutinized and commented on all of them. This has represented a substantial and sustained effort on their part for which we are extremely grateful. Higher education attached priority to having AS levels in mathematics, English, modern languages and design and technology. I am pleased that in the first year there has been a particularly good take-up in these subjects. Not surprisingly, many students are doing computing, but a good proportion of those doing modern languages are boys; an improvement on the balance we find at A level.

My view is that there are probably too many syllabuses and I hope that early on in its life the new SEAC will take this on board so that we have a smaller range of syllabuses which genuinely meet the differing needs of students for contrasting or complementary study.

To sum up: the government is backing AS levels and it is now up to schools, colleges and higher education to make a success of this policy. Higginson ended his report with a reference to the challenge facing the UK in 1992 when barriers to competition between EC member states are removed. He said:

> Employers will depend increasingly on people ... who can apply themselves effectively to a new range of tasks, who can speak other languages and who can work with confidence and independence ... At the same time, the system must respond to the talents and circumstances of the student.

We believe that AS levels will help equip our young people to meet that challenge. It is now up to you.

Reference

DEPARTMENT OF EDUCATION AND SCIENCE (1988) *Advancing A Levels: Report of a Committee appointed by the Secretary of State for Education and Science and the Secretary of State for Wales*, (The Higginson Report), London, HMSO.

Discussion on chapter 7

Mr. Taylor You suggested that schools might adopt AS levels by putting them in the timetable of the general studies slot. In schools, such as mine, where we have a very broad ranging advanced general studies programme, a pupil might then finish up doing perhaps one AS level instead of a wide range of subjects. The curriculum will not therefore be broadened by the introduction of AS.

Mr. Jackson My remit does not include schools but I will do my best to deal with this and other schools' questions. In answer to the last question, it seems to me that there is clearly a risk involved and that balances have to be struck. These are rather obvious things to say. What I guess we are asking you to do is to look at actual timetabling and your distribution of subjects with the facilities you have available, and see how best you can promote AS levels. We think it is in your interest, the students' interest and the country's interest to do that. There are going to be all sorts of ways in which you can do it. Some people may not be able to do it. One of the ways is to look at general studies and you will have to consider the trade-off between the one AS or the broad range of things that do not actually lead to a qualification, and perhaps may not be pursued with the same kind of seriousness and intensity as an examination subject. I have the impression that kids are very motivated by examinations — perhaps too motivated by them — and maybe it is part of your philosophy to try to stop them being excessively motivated. I see you nodding. But on the other hand it may be that your policy is not guaranteed 100 per cent success so it could be that your trade-off includes greater performance in the examined subject than you might be getting in the broader non-examined course. These are things that you have got to decide upon with reference to local circumstances in your own school and LEA; it cannot be decided upon by anyone else. We are simply making recommendations as to how you can try and fit this examination into the new system.

Mr. Davies I am a bit worried about the proliferation of examinations. I wondered if you are not equally anxious on that ground with the introduction of AS levels. Because although you urge that they are not intermediate levels we can never guarantee one hundred per cent that this is not so. I could well see very solid reasons for entering a youngster for an AS course wherever his chances of success at A level seem to be in doubt. Also you claim that the universities will be discouraged from admitting youngsters who have taken AS levels after one year. I doubt whether the universities will be discouraged from admitting someone who has, say, got a grade A in AS level maths simply on the grounds that he took the examination at seventeen. Against the background of schools spending at least a third of their capital for students on examination entries — and that figure would be doubled if one includes GCSE — I wondered if the economic factors might not be something that your headmistress might take seriously?

Mr. Jackson I believe it is really quite remarkable and positive that right at the head of government we have somebody who has taken the kind of very close interest that occasionally emerges in the press. There was a time when Prime Ministers simply were not interested in education; it was a low priority subject, and a matter of no great significance. You could have the only woman member of the Cabinet doing that job. But it is now the very serious stuff of high politics, and that must be a good thing. One of the consequences of that is, of course, the evolution of ideas and tests and examinations and methods of assessment. We are going through a period of ferment, that is one of the reasons why, as I was indicating in my speech, the government took a rather pragmatic view in relation to

Higginson; that maybe there was a danger of overloading the system with too much change at once, and that was one of the considerations leading to the rejection of the proposition that A levels should be shaded down. So we have to live through this period of ferment and debate and after it there will be a period of rationalization as people begin to identify successful practice. I think we can already see, to pick up your point, a need for rationalization of syllabuses as there has been, perhaps inevitably, a great explosion of these. They will need to be reviewed and consolidated and that is a very important task that we now face. But as far as AS levels are concerned I think a great deal will depend on the way it turns out in practice and the perceptions that people form of it. The concept is clear that AS levels are not an intermediate examination. AS is half of an A level and part of that is the idea that it should be a two year rather than a one year affair. If the punters respond in the way you describe, if AS becomes something for the not so academic child who you know is not really capable of doing a good job at A level, that will help to form perceptions of AS levels that will be damaging to it, and that would be a great pity if we want to use this as the device for broadening the curriculum at 18. That is the strategic objective: AS levels are the means that we think are appropriate at this stage to advance towards that objective. But the destiny of AS levels and the extent to which they can meet that strategic objective is very much in the hands of you, the providers, and depends on how you steer the system. We hope that the concept — which to us seems to be a good concept — of AS level being part of an A level rather than an intermediate stage, is one that will become established in practice through your efforts.

Mr. Austin I have considerable doubt about the credibility of offering AS subjects to my sixth form students. If I say to my sixth form students you can come in for a certain number of lessons and do half of the course on a teaching basis I am pretty certain the majority of the students — and their parents — will reject this. The obvious answer must therefore be to run AS courses on a free standing, independent basis, for which we need more resources and staff, and I think fundamentally this is what is lacking in the education system today. If you want all the change, and you want it to be successful and the schools to do the job that you are asking us to do — and you implied that now the government had backed AS's it is now up to the schools — then we need the resources. Give us the resources Minister and we will do that job for you.

Mr. Jackson Well, we do our best and maybe we could do better. We always get less than we ask for but we argue the case very forceably. There was in fact an 8 per cent increase in the resources available to the school system in the last PESC round; with inflation running at 4 per cent that is not a bad outcome. Yes, you can always make the case for more resources and we do make that case. But I am perfectly happy to defend the outcome, as I say 8 per cent seems to be a fairly good outcome in general. You say that you are not sure whether the students and their parents can be persuaded to accept AS levels. I think that if you believe that the curriculum should be broadened then it is up to you to persuade them. I mean there is a selling job to be done. Clearly something new like this requires a selling job and a positive attitude. If the feeling is we are not going to try and create any enthusiasm about this unless we get more resources then the consequence will be that something which is widely believed to be very desirable on educational grounds will not happen. That really would be a great pity. So I think it does require a positive attitude if you believe in breadth. I understand that there are different schools of thought and one respects that, but in the end higher education and employers will have their say and this will eventually feed back into the debate which is going on in the schools. But if you are committed to broadening the curriculum at 18 this is the vehicle to use, and it really has to be up to you to persuade people who may be a bit hesitant about something that is new to take the opportunity. We are doing our best to help.

Mr. Raeburn I welcome the introduction of AS as a means of providing an enriched and better balanced curriculum for the pupils at my school, some of whom are extremely able. This year I am providing for courses in ten subjects and it is hoped that this will generate over sixty subject entries in

1989. I have to say, however, that I see the introduction of AS levels as being an intermediary step for the more radical reform of A levels proposed in the recent report. My misgivings concerning the long-term suitability of AS levels remains despite this extremely interesting conference and the way in which the problems of AS were subjected to detailed analysis yesterday. Yesterday we heard a representative of examinations boards enlarge on the tremendous difficulties of reconciling the conflicting requirements, given their AS brief. Indeed, grappling with the fundamental question of whether half an A level is a meaningful concept at all. I must confess to great disappointment that talk of standards as low as they are at present should not have given place to the much more subtle and searching examination of the concepts of greater breadth and depth contained in the excellent Higginson Report. I do hope, Minister, that the dialogue will continue and that the proposal for a tougher and leaner A level programme of five subjects, which as a package does not seem to involve any devaluation of standards at all, will not be lost. At any rate the dialogue should continue.

Mr. Jackson You use the phrase that 'the dialogue should continue'. I used a phrase speaking in a conference last week 'the debate continues', and it obviously does. The evolution of the A level syllabuses, the kind of system that is appropriate in the light of the implementation of GCSE, the coming on stream of the national curriculum with the requirement for much greater breadth at 16, these are all questions which are not yet settled. What the government has done is to reject the specific proposals of Higginson, that is the leaner, fitter, tighter, diluted A level approach. But that does not seem to me to end the matter for all time. What it does, I think, is send a clear signal that for the moment, and for some time to come, the route to broadening at 18 is going to be AS levels. Although there are some problems with them we have got to find our way through them. That is the decision which government has made, rightly or wrongly. I think that when you see the wider context of GCSE, of the ferment which is taking place, of change through the system, one can understand why this is. I think one of the things one has got to understand is that for the world outside the education world there are very few landmarks. There are very few fixed points, very few things you can rest on. There is not a very accurate perception, or rather, a very intimate perception, of what is happening in schools. A levels are something that people know about, they do represent a landmark and I think that is one of the reasons why it is quite important to keep that landmark in place as we go through a process of change, change which does not yet command public support and confidence. We believe in GCSE and we are pushing it hard. But there is no doubt about it, there is a real concern and debate out there amongst the people who pay for it all, and the people who have children going through the system, about whether this is the right thing. We have not yet got public confidence about those things that are emerging from the ferment of change. A levels are something which we can hold on to as a recognizable landmark and I think that is one of those political factors in the situation. We want to pursue breadth though, this is the Higginson objective and we agree with it. AS levels are the instrument for that pursuit. I think it would be a great mistake, for example, to believe that Higginson will come back so there is no need to bother with AS levels. Or even worse, if we do not bother with AS levels then Higginson will have to come back. I think that that would be quite the wrong way to approach it. What we have to do is to try and make AS levels work. A level syllabuses will evolve, the system will evolve. These issues will not go away, they will be addressed progressively. They will be addressed in an evolutionary fashion, I think, rather than in a direct 'head-on' fashion.

Mr. Derbyshire I agree with what the Minister has just said and I believe that there is a way forward that will eventually unite AS with Higginson. I think there is one crucial step that this act of faith that we were talking about yesterday will require. That is a more flexible approval by those tutors who set the course requirements for university entry. We heard yesterday that the universities are already well pleased with their IB candidates and their Scottish candidates. If we could put pressure on those course tutors to accept the following then the problem would be resolved. Students would be invited to come to universities to take courses if they take three, four, five or six subjects post-16. If they only take three it would be natural to expect that all these would be at A level. If they take four, two would be at A level and presumably complementary. If they take five, and here is the act of faith, only one of them need be at A level, presumably, two others might be complementary. If six subjects are taken then the example recently set by Liverpool should be followed, that is all six could be at AS level. Market forces can be expected to help nudge higher education admissions policies in this direction but you, sir, could use your influence to help bring about this change. If admission requirements did change in the way outlined above, the differences between Higginson and AS levels would be resolved.

Mr. Jackson Thank you for that very positive way of putting it. I appreciate that. You raise some very interesting questions. Should government be intervening in or pre-scribing the method of entry to higher education? That is ground onto which I hesitate to tread. Not just because the universities are a powerful lobby, which indeed they are, but also because our system of higher education and its place in the national culture is very much bound up with the principle of autonomy. We understand and respect that. It is not the only way of running a higher education system, although so many people in Britain seem to think it is. The other day I was in the Netherlands where all the dons are civil servants and the physical capital is owned by the state. The things that the Dutch have been doing to reorganize their university system in the light of the same kind of pressures and interests that affect us make the changes that have been made in this country look like a vicarage tea party. We have to deal with, and want to deal with, proud, self-confident, autonomous institutions which regulate their own arrangements for teaching and research, and that must include the determination of their own admissions policy. We can exhort, we can encourage, we can influence, but I don't think we can direct. But of course market forces, to use the second limb of your argument, are a powerful ally in this. The fact is that higher education has been for many years a sellers' market, if you like to think of it in economic terms. The universities have been the seller, setting the price to government and successive governments have had to pay it. But more interestingly the universities have determined the conditions of entry into the activity which they supply. Nineteen per cent of qualified applicants for higher education in this country are turned away. So our higher education institutions have traditionally been in the business of selecting students rather than recruiting them. This has very interesting ramifications and implications which run through the whole system and I believe it is one of the reasons — I made a speech the other day about this — why we have relatively poor access, in the sense of social promotion, in higher education in Britain. I think that is a great pity. However, I must not digress. The point I come to though is that as a result of the demographic change there are going to be 35 per cent fewer 18-year-olds in 1995 than there were in 1980. Hopefully the economy will still be strong and expanding, with unemployment falling on the continuing trend.

Anyway, there is going to be a lot of demand for 18-year-olds, not just from higher education but also from employers. Higher education institutions will not only compete with employers but also amongst themselves. Since the funding of the system is going to be related to student numbers higher education institutions will be concerned to keep up their numbers. Government policy will be to try and sustain numbers in higher education, that is a clear commitment we made in our election manifesto to increase numbers to 1990, and the implication is that we want to try and maintain that kind of age participation rate after that time. So we are not looking forward to a fall in the numbers in higher education, although numbers are obviously going to reach a plateau. There is going to be a lot of competition to attract 18-year-olds into higher education, and between institutions to attract them to their institution rather than the one down the road. The polytechnics are, I think, going to put a lot of pressure on universities because one of the things that will flow from the changes that the Bill makes in respect of the evolution of polytechnics is certainly an enhancement of their status. With increasing recognition they will be seen as a more valid alternative to the university approach to higher education. There is therefore a lot of pressure coming on those notoriously conservative course tutors, to make them think seriously and deeply about the traditional routes into higher education, whether they can be modified and changed to their institution's advantage. Hopefully, the pedagogical philosophy concerning broadening and the instinct for institutional survival will actually bring about this sort of result that we both seem to be seeking.

Dr. Ingram Could I just say in that context that the CVCP has recently written round to all universities urging them to take access more seriously and reminding them that broader access has implications not only for admissions, but also from the way in which first year courses are taught. We are all, therefore, being urged to respond quickly and responsibly to the changes that lie ahead.

Dr. Burnet I have a responsibility for monitoring the effects of recent changes in science teaching and examining in schools with a view to introducing changes in the first year of university science courses. I was tremendously disappointed by what happened to Higginson because I feel that the things that have happened in GCSE are extremely good in terms of teaching science which, if coupled with changes at first year university level, would make it possible to recruit from a much broader spectrum of people in future. While the introduction of GCSE would eventually lead to a reduction in the content of A levels, so long as we in the universities changed our teaching methodology and first year courses, I felt that the change was for the better. I thought that Higginson provided a marvellous opportunity to achieve a slimming down of A levels, push the universities further down the road to structural change, and at the same time achieve a considerable broadening of the school curriculum. I thought it was a real opportunity to put all these things together and have more school leavers coming in to the universities with a broader education and finding it easier to link in to first year university science courses without having done A level. I did a survey of five schools sending students to the University of Kent back in February/March before the Higginson report was published. The strong message that emerged was; change your university course away from content and more towards process; Higginson is coming, a new age is dawning. What is your response to that Minister?

Mr. Jackson You are expressing disappointment and I am registering it. I do not really want to go over again what I have already said. Clearly, you and many others in the educational world have been thinking about these things in terms of a new age dawning. There are many people within the educational world who have misgivings and there are many more people out there who do not understand it — and in so far as they do understand, they do not like what they hear. We have got to recognize that that is a political reality and that the new age will not come about overnight. One recognizes that people do have misgivings and doubts. There are all sorts of different philosophies and different values that are relevant in this debate and maybe we do need time to knit them together as we go forward. While I recognize that there is a lot of disappointment in the educational world about the government's position on Higginson, there is not a lot more that I can add, except perhaps to say that it is not enough just to throw up your hands and say its terrible, the government's wrecked Higginson. It is a fact that the government does not favour the Higginson approach to broadening the curriculum, but there are other ways of skinning the cat. AS levels offer an alternative approach to the same strategic objective.

Dr. Burnet I just want to say that there are complications with AS levels. From the examples you are giving here from your booklet, there are people who will take a mixture of A and AS level. They will usually take an AS level as a subsidiary subject, maintaining, for example, their main science A levels. I do not see the sex balance in science being altered by the introduction of AS levels. There will still be a great deal to be done in terms of broadening and getting girls into science.

Mr. Jackson Of course there is a great deal to be done. That is exactly what we are all saying but it is early days. A great deal will depend on the commitment of you and your colleagues.

Mr. Langley I think we can safely say that we will be looking to AS levels to broaden the curriculum. But I have to say that I only decided to come to this conference after the government's reaction to the Higginson Report. We are looking to AS levels to make up that temporary deficit and I think we would see them as a temporary measure. One of our problems will be lack of resources to put on courses. I really do not think that we will be able, except in very few cases, to finance standard AS level courses. I think there will probably have to be an infeed into the first year teaching of A level programmes. Now that means that in a sense we have really got to reappraise the way in which we teach A levels. Subject by subject we have to examine the syllabuses and try to find out how we are going to do this. That is a major curriculum and staff development task. If the government is really serious about AS levels then staff development for AS levels will need to become a national priority and resources devoted to it. Only then will teachers be able to adequately reappraise how they teach A levels and how AS levels may be fitted into some kind of matrix or modular structure within A level programmes of study.

Mr. Jackson I think that is very helpful and I will certainly take note of what you have said. I will report back to my colleagues who are particularly concerned with schools policy.

Section V
Case Studies in Implemention

Chapter 8

The Experience of a Sixth Form College

D.L. Blake

South-east Essex Sixth Form College incorporated AS levels into its curriculum without much difficulty and in a way which fully conformed with the spirit behind their introduction.

Organizational Advantages

A large sixth form college has all the advantages necessary for introducing a new and largely unknown curriculum initiative. The larger the establishment the easier it is to subsidize, so that if in the first year it is necessary to have a small AS level set this is easily compensated for by slightly larger A level or GCSE sets elsewhere. Secondly, as well as having a large number of subjects on offer we have a large number of sets of most subjects so that it is possible to convert an A level set into an AS set without having to lose that subject from the curriculum. Thirdly, a major advantage of a sixth form college is the speed with which it can change the timetable; every year we are used to making changes in September in response to the changed choices of the new sixth form intake. As a result of these changes some planned sets are closed, other new sets are opened. There are no worries about having to fit in with a third form or a second form whose timetable slots may be fixed; a block structure to the entire timetable enables rapid adjustment to be made. Thus in 1987 when it came to committing staff time to AS levels we knew that it was a relatively simple matter to divert staffing if we were unsuccessful in recruiting students to AS levels.

Strategy

Having decided that AS levels were a worthwhile curriculum
initiative the first necessity was to decide on a strategy. Should we
introduce one or two subjects and then add one or two more each
year, or should we plan a major introduction? We settled for the
latter. We believed in the concept. We reckoned that this was one
way of broadening the curriculum, that there was a need for this
examination, and if that was the case then it was important for as
many students as possible to benefit. We were also aware that in
any new development there tends to come a take-off point when
suddenly everyone is involved. Teachers are only too well aware of
this when it comes to a new craze or fashion. We therefore tried to
provide as complete a programme as possible to try to break
through this take-off point in the first year. If you show that you
are committed by the number of courses that are being offered it is
much easier to sell the new examination to its clientele. With
relatively little persuasion, nearly all departments that were able to
decided to offer a course.

It was obviously a major risk doing this for many reasons. At
the time of this decision we did not know that all the subjects we
wanted to offer were going to have syllabuses ready and we were
aware that some of those syllabuses might not be exactly what we
wanted. We had no real idea of the demand from students as only
fifteen students had indicated an interest in AS levels on the
preliminary application forms. However, we were risking a known
amount of our staffing budget, only two-and-a-half per cent at
worst, and this was acceptable. We were not held back by a concern
about the ultimate acceptability of the examination, largely because
of the obvious commitment of the DES and the close links between
the Principal and Clive Wake of SCUE, which meant we were
aware of the rapidly changing attitude of the universities.

Marketing

The next main task was to market what we were offering. Any
new development which is introduced relatively quickly must be
marketed if it is to have any chance of success. Marketing does not
mean persuasion or pushing AS levels but ensuring that they are
properly understood and informatively considered by the students
and their parents.

We emphasized the very simple concept that an AS level is equivalent to half an A level. Whilst this may not be exactly true, many syllabuses involve more than half the work load, it is easy to understand and our parents, students and feeder schools readily accepted it. If a student is overloaded with work it is easy to make an adjustment at a later date. This concept also had the advantage of reinforcing the point that the new examination has the same status as A levels, i.e. the same standard but half the quantity.

We spent a lot of time advertising: we had parents' evenings, we gave out a special handbook, we used the DES glossy, the SCUE booklet and we had displays. Each of our students receives an extended interview in September with their personal tutor to finalize courses so it was important that all college staff were aware of the implications of AS levels, and could give informed advice irrespective of their personal opinion.

We spent some time identifying a number of markets for AS levels. One of these was the large group of students who have problems with the choice of a third A level. Whilst many students may know what they want to do, a potential doctor wanting chemistry, physics and biology for example, more are uncertain of their choice of third subject, or even second subject. With AS levels, when a student is in a dilemma as to which of two subjects to take as a third subject the tutor has the opportunity of saying 'why not do both?'. This adds a new dimension to the discussion. Obviously in some students' eyes taking an AS level instead of an A level reduces the risk of taking a subject which they are not sure about; this would give them the confidence to try new subjects, including perhaps an important subject like mathematics on which they might not have risked a full A level. Some students would welcome the opportunity to take an interesting fourth subject, they would not want the commitment of a full A level but an AS would be acceptable.

Clearly students with particular complementary or contrasting needs are a potential market but in general we did not see their needs being met by adding an AS level to a programme of three A levels. We felt that a course of three A levels plus an AS level should be reserved for above average students only; we were far happier for others to take two AS levels instead of a third A level. We did not want to sacrifice any of our extensive non-examination general education programme, and there was the obvious possibility of overloading a student.

Another group of potential takers are those students who will find it hard to cope with three A levels. They have traditionally followed a course of two A levels, with two O levels in each of the sixth form years. We thought it a much better examination curriculum to start with two A levels, one AS level and one GCSE.

There was a potential group taking one AS level with four GCSEs. This was seen to be a small market. Their main objective in the college is to increase their tally of GCSEs and many will start on A levels the following year. The AS level gives them a variation from GCSE work, a taster of A level standard work and some encouragement to continue with full time education at the end of the year. Some of these students would start a full A level programme at the end of the year alongside their continuing AS course, others would start A level in that subject, the AS year not being wasted as it would have provided an excellent foundation and prevented the student losing touch with that subject. This was thought to be especially useful for mathematics.

Guidelines on Combinations

Table 1 is a copy of the college's basic guidelines on the combination of AS levels with other examinations. In no case in the first year were we recommending students to take more than two AS levels though this will clearly change in the future. It seemed prudent to limit any risk in the short run.

Table 1: *Guidelines on AS combinations. South-east Essex Sixth Form College*

A AS GCSE	
3 + 1 + 0	a) Students should have a substantial number of GCSE passes with a significant number of higher grades.
	b) One contrasting subject, not necessarily the AS, should be recommended.
3 + 2 + 0	a) A special case when one of the A levels is Further Maths.
	b) This will give the same overall time commitment as the example above. It also provides a fall-back position if Further Maths proves too difficult.
2 + 2 + (?)	a) This is the equivalent of three A levels.
	b) Normal entrance requirements for A level are expected.
2 + 1 + 1	a) This may become the normal pattern for those qualified for only two A levels.
	b) The course entrance requirement is 4 grade C passes.
0 + 1 + 4	a) For those with 3 grade C passes only.
	b) Higher grade pass required in the subject chosen or refer to head of department.
	c) This course will terminate at the end of one year if the student leaves or fails to qualify as an A level re-entrant.

Note: For the time being it would be considered unwise for a student to study more than two AS levels.

In 1987 it was not possible to do an AS level in only one year; however when it is possible it is not the intention of the college to enable students to complete an AS course in the lower sixth, especially not en route to A level. This rule might be relaxed for upper sixth students who for some reason or other might need an extra subject after one year but it is not expected that there will be many such students.

We considered the question of complementary or contrasting subjects. If the planned programme of subjects involved more than three subjects at A or AS level students were encouraged to consider a contrasting subject, although it was not necessary for this to be the AS level. This would still leave three complementary subjects.

Examining the programmes chosen by students is illuminating in this regard. The contrasting subject is obvious in the following examples:

A physics   A chemistry   A biology   AS French
A mathematics   A chemistry   A biology   AS English

and the complementary nature of the following are also clear:

A mathematics   A biology   A chemistry   AS physics
A English   A history   A theatre studies
AS classical civilization.

But programmes such as these were a minority of the total that were taken up. In the great majority of cases it is very difficult to be so precise. For example with the combination:

A geography   A economics   AS mathematics
AS French

is the French complementary or contrasting? Or, alternatively, with

A economics   A mathematics   AS history
AS psychology

which, if any, of these subjects is complementary or contrasting? Most programmes are not easily classified. Many subjects such as geography, psychology and mathematics have close links with a wide spectrum of disciplines. Students are able to make their programmes of courses as broad as they wish. Besides, increasingly students have been selecting a wider range of A level subjects in combination.

In setting up our courses we also treated AS as half an A level.

Thus the entry requirements for a whole programme or a particular course were the same as for A level. The teaching time we gave to each course was also half that given to A levels although our blocking system permitted up to three hours each week. Most subjects, but not all, have found this sufficient, though teaching method may be as important as size of syllabus as far as this is concerned. Each of the four A level option blocks were divided in half to give two AS option blocks, maximizing the possibilities of subject combination. In nearly all cases the AS is taught completely separately from the A level.

Numbers and Subject Range

We started the academic year 1987–88 with 117 students following at least one AS course, about 25 per cent of the lower sixth A level cohort, (see table 2). Approximately a quarter of the AS students were following a programme of three A levels and one AS level; a quarter two A levels and one AS level and the majority of the remainder two A levels and two AS levels.

Table 3 shows the range of subjects which were able to start in September 1987 and the number of students in each case. There were three sets of mathematics, to be consolidated into two, and two of English. The choices inevitably reflect the nature of the area in which the college is located and the patterns of subject choice which have built up. Despite its uneconomic size it was considered worthwhile continuing with French as languages are in need of encouragement, but other subjects such as biology and chemistry which had been on offer did not get off the ground. Other subjects with small numbers were taught with A level groups. It is interesting to note how successful some of the 'new' subjects — such as psychology and sociology — have been in recruiting to AS

Table 2: *Number of students taking at least one AS level course September 1987, South-east Essex Sixth Form College*

	Male	Female	Total
One AS	30	33	63
Two AS	29	24	53
Three AS	1	0	1
Total	60	57	117

Note: Total A-level cohort, 1987 entry: 475 students.

Table 3:   Range of AS subjects chosen September 1987, South-east Essex Sixth Form College

	Male	Female	Total
Mathematics	15	11	26
English	11	13	24
Art (stage design)	0	3	3*
Classical civilization	1	8	9
Economics	3	3	6
Electronics	6	0	6
French	1	4	5
Geography	4	4	8
Geology	5	4	9
History	5	7	12
Physics	11	3	14
Political studies	9	3	12
Practical music	1	2	3*
Psychology	8	10	18
Sociology	7	11	18
Total			173

*   taught with A level

courses, with no reduction in the number of students selecting them at A level.

Table 4 shows the growth of interest in AS levels. The possible thirty examination entries indicated before September 1987 turned into 173 by the end of the registration period, and we already have more than 220 requests for AS courses in the academic year 1988–89, a number which is bound to rise again at registration. Students show much enthusiasm for AS levels, they welcome the extra choices provided. The college's strategy seems to have paid off and in the first year of their introduction it is fair to say that AS levels have been a considerable success.

Postscript: The Position in September 1988

The number of students continuing with at least one AS subject into the upper sixth has fallen from the original 117 students to

Table 4:   Numbers of students on AS courses expressed as subject entries, South-east Essex Sixth Form College

Applications by end of March 1987	30
Registrations September 1987	173
Applications by end of March 1988	218

eighty-seven, with 115 subject entries. This is a much larger percentage fall than with A level classes and the largest fall has been in the group taking one AS with three A levels. Considering all their commitments they have found their work load too great, at least compared with their peers. None of those students regretted studying only half an AS course. Students who saw two AS subjects as a direct replacement for one A level have been the most stable group. Several students dropped an AS to take up the A level in the same subject when they found how interesting it was.

The new lower sixth has seen 193 students out of an A level cohort of 563 start at least one AS level. This could result in 298 subject entries. This is a substantial increase on 1987 even when taking into account the larger cohort. Several subjects have been added to the choice available for the new student intake, of these art and computing have been particularly successful in recruiting classes. The number taking economics had to be limited because of excessive demand. Two sets have begun in English, electronics, computing and art, and three in mathematics.

Chapter 9

The Comprehensive Experience

T.M. Axon

If I can just sketch in something of the background. I come from an average comprehensive school in Swindon, with a medium-sized sixth form of about 130, that is upper and lower sixth together, and most of those are A level students. In our lower sixth we have sixty A level students at the moment. Many of those would be taking three, some four, and some would be taking two A levels. For some time there has been a drive from staff to broaden our A level programme. But we wanted to do it in a certificated way. We had examined the International Baccalaureate and we had seriously considered moving in that direction. We had in fact gathered quite a lot of materials, but we discovered that the government were thinking of introducing AS levels and we decided to look at those instead. We were also aware that there might be problems for GCSE students when they reached A level courses. We thought that the current courses really were not sufficiently innovative for these GCSE students. We had heard the government was going to do something about broadening the sixth form curriculum with courses suitable for ex-GCSE students, but we saw no evidence of it at the time. So the staff of Ridgeway thought they would like to try to find a way of doing it themselves.

We had to address various factors before we could introduce the system we are currently using for AS levels. We had to persuade students and parents and governors and other staff that it really was worth doing. I am not going to spend any time on that because David Blake (see chapter 8 in this volume) has already explained some of the techniques that he used and I am sure we all have our own ways of doing things. What was interesting was that the process was surprisingly unrocky. We did not have any problems persuading people that AS was worth doing even though at that time back in 1986 we were not sure that universities and employers would accept AS levels. We were doing it purely for certificated broadening. We then had to find the resources to mount the new courses and find acceptable syllabuses — the SEC agreed syllabuses simply were not available at that time. How did we solve these problems? Since I am not sure that we have solved them all perhaps the question ought to be rephrased: 'How did we attempt to solve them?'

We did a fairly massive exercise with university admissions tutors to find out whether they would accept AS levels or not. We were fairly convinced that an awful lot of them would not at that stage. Having said that, SCUE has done a marvellous job in the meantime and we do believe now that the huge majority of admissions tutors will accept AS levels. They actually now know what AS levels are and they will accept them instead of various combinations of A level. We are fairly convinced of that and therefore do not have too many worries on that score.

The Modular Approach

Resourcing was the major problem. We are in a shire county and in the current vernacular we are not in a 'loads-a-teachers' metropolitan region or the 'pots-a-money' independent sector. Perhaps we are in a 'bags-a-challenge' county area. We wondered about scrapping general studies or reducing it and providing a couple of AS courses instead. That is probably a possibility for most comprehensive schools with our size of sixth form, though whether it is educationally desirable is another matter. I was very struck by Robert Jackson's comment this morning that in requiring the same standard of work but only half the study time he thought AS levels should be locked into A levels. We took that view independently earlier on. Various staff committees got together and came up with what is an administratively simple theoretical model for solving the problem. A so-called n and n over 2 model, where n is the number of modules that go to make up the A level course, and n over 2, of course, being half the number of modules, i.e., the number contained in the AS course. Why did the staff come up with that solution? There was certainly quite a lot of interest in the modular curriculum at the time. Peter Watkins, in his Schools Curriculum Development Council conferences on the modular curriculum, had given a very wide-ranging review of the advantages and disadvantages of the modular approach and our staff were aware of these. The modular approach had in fact been pioneered by a school in Wales and one in Oxford called Peers School. A Technical and Vocational Education Initiative (TVEI) group in Peterborough had already started work on this kind of model, being funded by TVEI, and a little later a TVEI group in Somerset began working in a similar way. They have developed in a different way since. So the approach is not original, but it did seem to us to offer a more efficient use of resources, particularly staff resources, because we could resort to concurrent or co-teaching of A and AS level students. In other words, both would study to the same depth and AS would not be an easy option. Theoretically class sizes would increase because both would use the same books and equipment. Perhaps most important of all, it allowed us to produce our own syllabuses and assessment could be designed to fit in with GCSE assessment methods. We have heard it said that we had simply joined the Gadarene rush into modules. That is a matter of opinion; we took the view that the modular pattern was a perfect organizational solution to the goal we had set ourselves, namely to achieve a broadening in our curriculum. How otherwise could we have introduced AS levels when we really did not have the staff to put on free-standing AS levels, except in one or two subjects?

Syllabuses and Assessment

We took our scheme to the University of London School Examinations Board and the Deputy Director and staff there really were most positive and encouraging about the whole idea. They were very helpful but critical friends and they have been very helpful in terms of administration. They provided moderators in every one of the seven subjects that we decided to adopt and I cannot praise them too highly. The Secondary Examinations Council (SEC) gave provisional approval (pilot status) for 1989 and 1990 on Sir Wilfred Cockcroft's (chairman's) action, and that is where we stand at the moment.

Our courses started last September and module 3 is just ending. The staff wrote their own syllabuses but most were based on University of London material. That seemed to us to be a sensible way of handling it at that stage. We did not want to wait until September 1988: the staff drive was there; the momentum was there for a start and so we 'got on with it'. There was a greater likelihood of getting SEC approval if we used material from existing approved syllabuses. In the event they were not all based on existing approved syllabuses but they have all gone through for the moment. Each syllabus met with A level common 'core' requirements. You will know that you can get hold of a book on common 'core' material from any examinations board and it tells anybody designing an A level syllabus exactly what the universities are looking for in a whole range of subjects.

The methods of assessment were broader than the traditional A level assessment. We did move towards the GCSE model which includes coursework and other forms of assessment. We produced our own assessment material and examination papers, but everything was moderated by board moderators. Initially we found that our staff were writing syllabuses that were far too hard and far too full. They tended to be more like S level syllabuses, or beyond. Those of you who are examiners perhaps know the problem that arises when you are asked to say whether it is 'hard', 'average' or 'easy'. You may think a question is 'average' but find it is impossible for students in practice. That was the kind of difficulty we had in writing these syllabuses. There was initially far too much assessment also. That has now all been reduced, but there may still be somewhat too much of both in one or two of the syllabuses.

Numbers Taking AS

The number of students taking AS courses when we started in September 1987 are given in table 1. The relatively small numbers asking for AS levels — just twelve people in September — may need some explanation. AS levels were new, and we were not really convinced at the time that the universities would accept them and so we did not market AS as something everyone should go for. What we did was to start the scheme in the hope that in future years we would have fairly large numbers going for AS if the universities accepted it.

What has happened since can be seen from the second column of table 1; clearly, the number taking AS has declined. The third column shows the number of A level students we have in those particular subjects which are modularized; we have rather more in traditional A level subjects. Column four shows the reasons why enrolments on AS courses have declined. Three students have

Table 1:   *Modular A/AS Student Numbers at the Ridgeway School*

	Start of course AS students	Now July 1988 AS students	Modular A students	Reason for change
Biology	3	2	16	1 left
Economics	2	1	21	1 dropped subject
English	3	1	26	1 converted to A
				1 dropped subject
				1 left
French	0	0	5	
Geography	3	0	19	2 converted to A
				1 dropped subject
History	0	0	6	
Religious education	1	0	4	1 left
TOTAL AS	12	4		

converted from an AS course to an A level course; three students have simply dropped an AS course, and three students have dropped out of the school; this latter group includes one individual who happened to be taking three modular AS courses. No statistical conclusion can be drawn from these figures, they are derived from far too small a sample.

However, the figures do point in certain directions and that is helpful to us. They suggest that many students now want to do four A levels. In that first column we could have had some more, but people in fact had looked at the possibility of doing three A levels plus an AS and had decided they would not do that, they would take 4 A levels instead. Now up until this year our four A level students were always the double mathematics people. This year we have got a variety of four A level students because they had thought about doing an AS first. I think it is regrettable that so many people want to do four A levels, at least as A levels currently exist. Next year it looks as though we are going to have rather more starting AS courses, particularly in English and French, and in both English and French we expect them to be mainly contrasting subjects. Something like nine people have put down to do English — and they all tend to be primarily mathematicians and scientists. In the case of French, the same thing is happening and that shows not only good marketing by the teachers concerned, but also a recognition from students, at last, that these subjects are important. We are also going to be running a mathematics AS level, by the way, but not in this scheme. In terms of contrasting and complementary, we identified three choices as contrasting, two as complementary, but, as David Blake has said, most of them were neither.

The Maturation Effect

We have encountered some problems, in particular the so-called maturation effect. Perhaps mistakenly, pre-16 modular courses tend to take no account of student maturation from 14–16 years. We think that maturation cannot be ignored when assessing students of 16–18 years of age because we believe a student changes significantly over these two years. We have to take account of maturation because young people's understanding of the world is broadening at a tremendous rate at that stage of life. We have to find a way of dealing with that. As far as we know there has been little or no research to date on the maturation effect and how to take account of it when assessing students in this age range. How then do we arrive at a final A level grade in a modular A level system? There is no recognized procedure and it is a major issue for us. We started by thinking in simplistic terms of an addition of modular scores, but very soon realized that was not going to work in a way that could take account of maturation or of the varying discriminatory qualities of different forms of assessment. Dr. Kingdon, who is here, is helping very considerably by undertaking research on how we might find a solution to this problem.

Having said that, I can imagine a number of people thinking 'what an irresponsible school for starting something to which they don't know the answer — they don't know how it will end up at the end of the day'. I can only counter such thoughts, and the arguments that they might give rise to, by reminding you that any bold, or imaginative or innovative change is described thus simply because at the time the change occurred the consequences of it were not precisely known, or beyond dispute. Furthermore, I can assure you that we do have tremendous support from a number of people and organizations at this stage, despite the difficulties. SCUE have been to visit and have declared themselves very interested indeed and were enthusiastic about the possibilities. Peter Dines from SEC has been to look at what is going on, together with a whole host of other people. We have got support. We are also a school that up to now has had a consistently good A level record in terms of public examinations successes. We would not expect that record to be any less good in a year's time than it has been over the years; indeed, we hope the modular courses will enhance it. So, because we have safety nets and are recording every conceivable element of assessment at the moment, we are prepared to delay a solution to the problems of maturation and of a method of arriving at a final grade until early in the next academic year. We have some ideas but now is perhaps not the time to go into them. Students do have feedback on how they get on in a module. They are told what grade they would be likely to attain if they continued working at that level of effort and quality for the remainder of the course. They are not given any raw scores from any forms of assessment.

Other Difficulties

There have been other difficulties. For example, the work load on teachers has been tremendous. You can probably imagine the work involved in designing the courses initially and then providing all assessment materials and examinations for each module well in advance. These are facts and not complaints but the scheme that we have embarked upon is certainly not for the faint-hearted. We would prefer to see London providing all the examinations at the end of the module and the school providing all the coursework, and that is something for the future. Assessment design seems to be harder in a modular scheme at this level than it would be in a scheme in which the assessment comes at the end of a two year course, when there is a wider span of topics from which to choose. There are extra problems in collecting material and limiting assessments to module content.

A point on assessment practice is worth mentioning. If one uses innovative methods of assessment you have to train the students beforehand and we had overlooked this. For instance, if an assessment involves an oral presentation of an extended essay, which student has got the skill to do that without training? Precious few, it seems.

Some staff feel time bound. For example, the very good department of economics that we have feels it cannot move outside the planned module material to talk about emergent current economic issues. We hope we can overcome this particular problem.

Time lost gives rise to other problems. What happens if a teacher falls ill for two weeks or so, or one of the students falls ill for three weeks? Both have happened and we had to cope — with luck, extra lunchtime lessons and by extending module time into a planned 'buffer zone'. Do not put biology and geography fieldwork into the same module time. We did — it really was a little crass! We have just appointed a co-ordinator of supported self-study to help with some of the problems here. Administration has to be perfect in a modular scheme of this sort. You cannot afford to let anything go wrong that could have been foreseen. And you have to try and foresee everything, every little detail.

Relationships with moderators are a key element of success. Where the relationships are not of the highest quality, you have a source of potential difficulty. Where they are excellent then lines of communication are usually open and any difficulties can be squashed in infancy. Thus good relationships with moderators are essential for a scheme of the kind that we have introduced. Another problem that we have discovered in the most recent module is that some students have started giving in some coursework late — not a problem we had anticipated. It did not happen in the first two modules and we now need a strategy for dealing with it.

The Benefits

What about the advantages? Motivation really is extraordinary at the moment. It is the best lower sixth we have had, ever, in terms of real interest in what is going on in the classroom. We have had some good ones, but the current one is the best ever, though academic ability *per se* is no better than it was in some of the other good years we have had. It is all down to motivation and this year motivation has really taken off. Students gear up very quickly indeed to A level work, they work steadily throughout the year. They are not waiting until the end of the second year until they really get down to it. They are working hard right from the start. They were mildly frightened about the first modular assessment in the autumn term, but once they overcame that bit of stress they really did feel good and we found that the quality of their thinking, their questioning and their writing has been far superior to anything we would have expected from that age group in the past. In terms of innovation for our staff, it really has facilitated staff debate, development and progression, and the enthusiasm that it has engendered has spilled over into various other areas of the school. In terms of evaluation, it has stimulated us to examine right across the curriculum what is being taught, and why, and how. As a result

Table 2: *Modular A/AS Students at Ridgeway School*

	Start of Course AS Students	Modular A Students
Biology	2	12
Economics	1	26
English	5	18
French	1	11
Geography	2	28
History	0	5
Religious education	0	0
TOTAL	11	100

of this we have built a number of different skills and techniques into the curriculum as a whole. There is of course effective monitoring by the students themselves of their own performance, and that cannot be undervalued. Altogether, the advantages really do far outweigh the difficulties which we have encountered — but these we think will be soluble. In conclusion: for a school with a relatively small sixth form which is committed to broadening education at that level we believe this model has a lot to offer.

Postscript: September 1988

The numbers on modularized A and AS courses for those *entering* the sixth form in September 1988 are shown in table 2. Although the absolute number of registrations for AS courses is not high, it is about the same as for September 1987. Bearing in mind that there are about sixty-eight students in the lower sixth, this still suggests a 20–25 per cent increase in broadening attributable to the modular A level scheme.

Discussion on chapters 8 and 9

Conference member   Could Mr. Blake tell us how his school managed to fund the introduction of AS levels? If this was achieved through rearranging resources, was this done without damaging other areas of work?

Mr. Blake   We decided that in the first year we were prepared to commit about three per cent of our staff time towards it and then we closed down other courses in order to release this staff time. In some cases we had to reallocate part-time staff to compensate but we achieved all the changes necessary at the same time as losing five members of staff because of falling rolls. It was a matter of saying to departmental heads that they had to find this time, by dropping existing courses or by taking on more students with existing staff. We were able to do it because we are a large school.

Conference member   I don't suppose you had to close down many A level classes?

Mr. Blake   Relatively few, but we did have to close down some. We looked particularly closely at our GCSE classes which in quite a number of cases were slightly more generously staffed than we thought necessary. So the whole of the rest of the curriculum lost. As any timetabler knows, there are always occasions when it gets to the point where one has to stand firm and say 'No, you have got to have one set instead of two'. We did that sort of thing.

Conference member   Can I ask about the actual relationship between theory and practice. You said in your talk about wanting to preserve general studies. We adopted a similar approach saying that while general studies would be preserved we would be prepared to sacrifice an A level set or allow GCSE sets to take slightly larger numbers if necessary, and so on. In practice, it looks as though things might not work out quite like that, and it may well be that in the end general studies cannot be maintained, although it has not disappeared yet.

Mr. Blake Although it seems incredible, we actually managed to increase the number of options in general studies, perhaps because we cut away a little bit too much on the other courses. What you are saying is right. The group from which we are losing students — and we have lost students in exactly the same way as they have at Ridgeway — has tended to be that group doing three A levels plus one AS course. In order to carry such a load students in this group would have to reduce their general studies commitment, substituting instead another two and a half hours of examination work. The group which is most secure, which we are most happy with, and for which development continues, is without doubt the two A plus two AS group. Fall out from the two A plus one AS group has been no greater than fall out in the past from the two A group. In our experience it is the student who does an AS on top of his three A levels who is most likely to abandon his AS subject when he discovers it involves too much work.

Conference member I have been following the development in modular A levels and one particular aspect of it worries me, namely the problem of discontinuity. Is there not a serious problem of discontinuity when you have students opting into and out of modules within a given subject area?

Mr. Axon I did not describe how this scheme works, but we do have a booklet which tries to explain the way in which that issue is addressed. There is a basic or foundation module for all A and AS level students. Take for instance economic principles. There is a module simply on economic principles and after they have taken that students can then choose two of the remaining five modules if they are AS, but there is a set of rules which means that they will have a coherent course. The staff who produce the syllabuses and the staff at the University of London feel that the way it has been handled so far is facilitating the development of coherent courses. I am not entirely convinced myself, in at least one of the subjects, that that is the case and I suspect that there might well be the kind of discontinuity that you have asked about. But the syllabuses are being developed all the time, and hopefully the problem in that subject will also be resolved.

Conference member Within your modular structure do students in the lower sixth take the same modules as students in the upper sixth, or are they taught separately?

Mr. Axon We did set the scheme up in such a way that the upper and lower sixth could be taking the same modules. That was the original intention but we are not going to be doing it next year. In fact, we find that at the moment we do have sufficient resources to repeat modules in most subjects. Indeed, the only subject for which repetition is not possible is one which, so far at least, has no takers next year.

Conference member Do AS students find that there are gaps between modules?

Mr. Axon Yes there will be gaps between modules of most AS levels, and we have some tactics for dealing with transfer between separated AS modules. We thought of fitting in some other kind of certificated course, perhaps one of the RSA II courses, in those gaps and we are attempting to do that at the moment with some students, though not all. But we are in all cases saying that near the end of the gap something like two hours, which is about 5 per cent of the time spent on a module, should be spent on an individualized study, a set assignment, or in a student self-help group or short recapitulatory course. So, after finishing one module there is a gap lasting as long as a module — except for the two hours of study — before the next one begins. And that is working quite well.

Section VI
Further Discussion and Comment

Chapter 10

General Discussion

Professor Hughes   The purpose of this session is to give you an opportunity to ask any questions that you might not have been able to ask during the earlier sessions, or to ask further questions about those issues that you think were not sufficiently well covered in the earlier sessions.

Ms. Shaw   The issue I would like to raise is that of ethos. I think A level examinations have always been very content-based and I believe that Higginson, in addition to wanting to reform the curriculum, wanted to make it a more processed based curriculum. I would like to know if any of the current AS syllabuses, including Mr. Axon's modular approach, are attempting to do that. In my view that is the only way that GCSE and post-16 courses can become compatible.

Conference member   For some time now the general trend in A level syllabuses has been away from A levels being just a collection of facts to be learnt; instead there has been an increasing emphasis on process. In some subjects this trend towards process has been happening more quickly than in others. This is one of the instances where I think Higginson and other reports — because it is certainly not something that is restricted to Higginson — picked on something that is already happening, drew attention to it and then talked about ways in which it might be advanced and furthered. Mr. Axon in his talk held up the common-core booklet which was produced by the GCE boards in association with SCUE and CVCP etc., and in that document you will also see quite a strong shift away from defining the common core in terms of content, and an increasing emphasis on skills, approaches and processes.

Mr. Rogers I would like to ask a question to which I have not yet heard a satisfactory answer. It is related to the handouts that we got from Dr. Kingdon and concerns AS level mathematics. We are told that the widely-used AO level syllabuses are going to be withdrawn even though many schools still wish for a one-year fifth form course for students who take GCSE early. It is claimed that the syllabuses in pure maths and in pure maths and theoretical mechanics are designed so that they may be taught as a one-year course, if that is desired. We have heard about the maturation effect on AS level and that AS level is intended as a two year event. But in the case of the mathematics courses mentioned above we are told it can be taken as a one-year course. What do you feel about students in the fifth year taking AS level mathematics, particularly when the schools claim that many of the students do have the required maturity to study at an advanced level in that particular subject?

Dr. Kingdon I think there are some subjects where it is realistic to expect that some students will demonstrate a level of maturity within the subject context before they are eighteen years old, and I believe mathematics is one such subject. We have also seen it in subjects like computer studies, electronics and music. I think that if we talk about the performance required by a typical 18-year-old who has followed a course over two years, these are subject areas where from our experience good students do indeed have those sort of subject maturities, although I am not implying that they have other sorts of maturities as well. Therefore, that is one of the reasons why we have departed, very slightly, from the model. If the questioner has actually had an opportunity to look at some of the other syllabuses which we have offered, he will see that the mathematics one is something of an exception. We have tried to be realistic about existing patterns of sixth form provision, and fifth-form provision in the case of advanced courses, and tried to produce syllabuses that will fit in and adapt to something resembling the sort of structures we have today. And we have been fairly specific about the maths and acknowledged that users might not wish to stick too slavishly to the model which we think is appropriate for all of the other subjects. Now, with that in mind, it is clearly stated in those maths syllabuses which ones we feel could be used as one-year courses and for the good mathematicians who are going on to mathematics at other levels. While mathematics is rather a special case, I would like to make a more general point. Although the AS level is being thought of as a two year course with the examination at 18+, we appreciate that there will be schools which might want — in order to broaden the curriculum — to take AS levels in one year if that fits into their particular pattern of provision. We will observe what happens, during the early years of the examination, in order to learn what consequences follow from this particular approach to introducing AS levels into the curriculum.

Mr. Axon   Maths has proved to be a unique area. There are lots of problems associated with it. We are very keen, for example, to see the limited grade maths syllabus come through because some people get attracted to AS level maths thinking that if they cannot do the A level they might be able to cope with AS. That is wrong; I would rather see the weaker A level student doing a limited grade syllabus. There is no conflict between AS and limited grade mathematics; they are designed for different markets.

Conference member   I would like to ask Professor Wake about the development of the common core and the review of it. I am involved in the development of the new SMP 16–19 A level maths syllabus, which it is hoped will appeal to a much wider audience than the conventional syllabuses. At the moment the development of this new syllabus is constrained by the current common core. What is the process of reviewing the common core, and how soon can we hope for such a review?

Professor Wake   We are very aware of the fact that the common cores which were developed jointly with the CNAA a few years ago are now really out of date. As a result of our work on AS level syllabuses we have quite recently, in collaboration with the CNAA, set up a joint working party to look at the question of the future of common cores. Membership of this working party consists of representatives from CNAA, SCUE and the Association for Science Education. At the moment it is not the intention to sit down and work out new common cores, but rather to review the underlying principles. They are working very fast and we are hoping very much that there will be some kind of public statement early in the autumn. So things are being taken forward and we are hoping that there will be some progress with that element of the Higginson Report which referred to common cores.

Mr. Brenchley Can I ask Mr. Blake if he has done any work on forecasting examination entry; and also whether he or Mr. Axon is considering how they might tackle a potential growth in examination costs when local financial management is introduced.

Mr. Blake The simple answer is no, but we are intending to do so for reasons of local financial management. Heretofore the County has paid for all examination entry fees. The position is liable to change and so we will look at it. We have not got anywhere yet, I am afraid.

Mr. Axon This is a very good question because if you look at pre-16 modular schemes they are likely to cost considerably more than traditional pre-16 courses, and once we have financial devolution that is going to be a real headache for schools, especially if we are not allowed to charge children for anything in schools. We have looked at fees in the modular A level scheme and we expect them to be exactly the same as they are for traditional A levels, at least at this stage. However, I think we have to be realistic. It is going to cost more in future because it costs more to administer any form of modular course. At the moment we are working on our local authority to try and persuade them, before financial devolution, to provide us with sufficient money to administer our programmes. So, although we have not got a solution at the moment, we are working on it.

Mr. Jones I was very heartened yesterday by Professor Wake's remark that he felt that in the majority of cases an AS level is effectively worth more than half an A level. I was therefore somewhat disheartened when he went on to say that on the points score system it would be given just half the weighting of an A level. What is the real value?

Professor Wake   I can only repeat what I said yesterday, that the points score system that has been devised for AS levels is based on the literal understanding of what an AS level is. Those of us who have worked with the AS level syllabuses, and those of you who have been teaching them, know very well that in some cases, perhaps in many cases, the syllabuses are still overweight in terms of content. But quite apart from that, as I said yesterday, it is clear that taking two AS level subjects instead of a single subject, especially if they are contrasting subjects, does put an extra burden on the individual. I am simply repeating what I said yesterday. Clearly it is very difficult to reconcile the way in which the points score system operates with perceptions of practitioners of the way AS levels are functioning at the moment. What we have done is to advise universities of this dilemma and suggested that they should be very flexible when it comes to the acceptance stage in August, even if they cannot bring themselves to make offers initially to AS candidates which are different in terms of points scores to those that they are making to straight A level candidates. I recognize that this is not very satisfactory. We are very dependent on the willingness of admissions tutors to do this but for the time being there is very little we can do about it. My own view, as I put it very firmly yesterday, is that the points score system is a most damaging process and the sooner we get away from it altogether the better. But that is still a battle that has to be fought. So I do not think I can satisfy you. I can simply explain what we are trying to do and acknowledge that we do accept there is a problem.

Conference member   Is it not possible, within the context of the points score system, that universities might be encouraged to adopt half points as part of a total which then clearly would be meaningless in an A level context. For example, two B's and a C at A level would be eleven points; if you were to offer a candidate ten and a half points the only way of achieving this score precisely would be if the grade in one of the AS subjects is one below what the corresponding A level grade would have been. In short, I am suggesting that lowering the overall requirements by half a point would mean accepting a C and D at AS level rather than a C at A level, or a B and C instead of a B.

Professor Wake   I see, yes. That sounds like a good idea; we will give it some thought.

Mr. Crossan   This is rather by way of a 'thank you' to the University for organizing this conference. When we came we were confused; then yesterday morning we were presented with a situation … a marriage, but in fact there are three parties in this marriage, ourselves, the boards and the universities. This fact reminded me of the story of the man who was married and went to a consultant to discuss his problems. The consultant said 'Of course, at the end of the first year you don't know who your wife is', and the man replied, 'I know who *she* is, but I've no idea who the hell I am'. During the past two days we have been told many things and some of what we have heard has confused us more in terms of our own identity in relation to AS levels than one would have thought possible. I wonder, in fact, if it might be possible for the university to produce a report on this conference. I realize that this will involve some expense but it has been a very beneficial conference and a permanent record of the proceedings would, I am sure, be of lasting benefit.

Professor Hughes   Given your opening remarks, I was relieved to hear what followed. It is our intention to try and get the proceedings of the conference published. If, in fact, we are unsuccessful in getting a publisher, then we will certainly look at the economics of publishing the proceedings ourselves.

Conference member   Mr. Chairman, I do not know whether I can speak for others but I think when I have finished you will be able to judge whether I am able to do so. I would just like to add to what the last speaker said by putting it on record that I have found this conference extremely useful. I am most grateful to the Vice-Chancellor, to you, your colleagues, academic, administrative and domestic, for all the arrangements that you have made for us. I found *all* the speakers apposite, clear and quite compelling, and I found them both complementary and contrasting. I found the accommodation comfortable; I must say when I arrived and saw the name 'Isobel' on my door, and I was hopeful. I was hoping that I would find here the some amenities, attractions and temptations that David Lodge so graphically described in *Its a Small World*, the world of higher education conferences. I waited up half the night and have to confess that I shall be unable to boast when I get home; on that score I was disappointed. But I do feel that, despite the queues in the dining hall, what we have been offered at the end of the queues has been excellent, too. We have had an opportunity to put our points to universities through SCUE, to yourselves in this University, to the examining boards and to the Minister. And for many of us for whom this has been a first visit, it has been good to see such a pleasant campus. I should just like to thank you all very much for putting this conference on.

Professor Hughes Thank you very much for those kind words. Perhaps this is the time to draw the conference to a close. I would like to end by thanking all of the principal speakers, some of whom are on the platform with me. To them and to the others who had to leave before the end of this conference I extend our thanks. But, of course, our main debt of gratitude goes to the 300 or so participants of this conference — to you. We always thought that there would be a lot of interest in a conference on AS and we were encouraged by the early responses that we had. In the end we had to turn many away because of the lack of places. I do hope that as a result of the discussion that took place yesterday we have managed to allay some of your fears about the attitude of university admissions officers. I think if there is a stereotype that has emerged from this conference, it is that of the conservative university admissions officer. Although I understand your fears and acknowledge that such conservatism does exist in some quarters, I assure you that we are doing all we can to combat it. At Kent we certainly do take AS levels seriously, as I think our prospectus shows. However, we are not complacent; we realize that we still have quite a number of changes to make before we can claim that our entry requirements fully reflect the arrival of AS levels. More generally, although it will take some time for both schools and universities to become fully confident about AS levels, I believe that confidence will come. The universities will have to take account of AS if only for reasons of self-interest. As they do, this will feed back into the schools and both teachers and students will increasingly accept the value of AS. I hope that this conference will play some part in bringing about the change of attitudes that is a necessary first step in this process.

Chapter 11

Concluding Comments

James J. Hughes

There have been several attempts over the past thirty years to broaden the sixth form curriculum. All of these attempts at reform, except one, have been rejected; only the AS proposal has been implemented. As Dr. Kingdon implied in his talk, the probable reason for this is that the AS proposal was the only one which did not pose a threat to A levels by seeking to replace them; instead it sought merely to supplement them. In his address to the conference Robert Jackson made it clear that the government supported AS levels because they are not an easy option but 'are locked into the A level system and thus provide a guarantee of quality to higher education and industry in line with known admission standards'. Indeed, one of the main reasons why the government rejected Higginson's proposal for five leaner, tougher A levels was because it did not believe that this could be achieved without loss of standards. Another reason was fear of overload on the school system following a period of substantial change.

The discussion and comment at the conference echoed that elsewhere, indicating that there is almost universal support for the Higginson proposals, outside of government, that is. However, it was equally obvious that there is strong support for a broadening of the curriculum and in arguing the government case Robert Jackson was adamant that this was to be achieved through the introduction of AS levels in all schools.

Under the existing A level system most students take three A level subjects together with a course in general studies or some other non-examined broadening course. There are deviations from this pattern, with some less able students taking a lighter load while more able students take a heavier one. For both weaker and more able students the existence of AS levels introduces other possible combinations which, on the face of it, might better suit their needs. For example, for an above average but not brilliant student three A levels plus one AS might be a more realistic programme than four full A levels. At the other extreme, two A levels plus one AS might be as much as a marginal student can cope with. Within the three A level model it will be possible to substitute two AS for one A level, thus ensuring a broader curriculum, particularly if one of the AS subjects is a contrasting one. Where four subjects or more are studied by all sixth formers this will make it possible for all science students to take a humanities or foreign language subject as well as three science subjects, and for a student studying the humanities to take a course in science or mathematics. This is not to be achieved by prescription but by counselling and guidance before sixth form studies begin.

Although the introduction of AS offers tremendous scope for broadening the curriculum, it will certainly not achieve this potential if its introduction is at the expense of some other broadening element in the curriculum. In short, if AS levels can only be mounted within a particular school by transferring resources away from general studies and other non-examined parts of the curriculum then any broadening that results will be more apparent than real. Such a transfer could occur if schools, keen to introduce AS, are denied additional resources to do so. When commenting on the difficulties that some schools would face in introducing AS levels Robert Jackson himself hinted that additional resources could not be taken for granted when he said that 'a fresh look at the disposition of time and resources in general studies and non-examined time could make all the difference'. In this he is certainly following Higginson who recommended that there would have to be some diminution of 'general time' if the five A level approach were to be adopted. However, it is important to stress that Higginson was not suggesting that all the additional time necessary to mount a five-subject programme should, or could, be provided from general time, or that general time should be reduced to zero. The comments of conference participants suggested that where they are already running successful general studies courses, they would be loathe to sacrifice these to make way for the intro-duction of AS.

When the DES and the Welsh Office first published the government's proposal on AS in 1984 they were quite adamant that their introduction would not require additional resources. The logic of this position would seem to imply that there is already some slack in the schools system, or that the new AS levels will replace existing courses, or the AS syllabuses can be devised in such a way as to make them co-teachable with A levels. It is quite clear from the comments of the representatives of examining boards that some AS syllabuses have been designed so as to be co-teachable, but certainly not all. Indeed, if the opportunities opened up by AS are to be fully exploited there will need to be some completely new, free-standing, syllabuses designed. Such courses will bring with them timetabling problems and will need to be adequately resourced.

Even where A and AS courses are taught together, thus economizing on teaching resources, there will be a need for a good deal of in-service training for teachers. As one participant put it, such training will not only enable teachers to reappraise their approach to teaching A levels, but will also encourage them to think how 'AS levels may be fitted into some kind of matrix or modular structure within A level programmes of study'. Although such training would not require resources to be devoted perman-ently to it, resources are certainly required during the early years of implementation. In addition, as was noted above, if AS levels are to achieve their full potential, without at the same time proscribing student choice, it will be necessary to devote further resources to counselling and guidance. It is therefore impossible to escape the conclusion that the successful transition to an A plus AS level system cannot be achieved without additional resources being devoted to sixth form studies. Whether or not such additional resources will be forthcoming will be one of the factors that determine how quickly, and how successfully, AS levels become integrated within the A level system.

While adequate resourcing is vital to the success of any new venture, resources themselves do not guarantee success. Attitudes and perceptions, particularly with regard to a new academic qualification, are also important. The first cohort of AS students will be taking the first AS examinations in the summer of 1989 and those proceeding to higher education will enter their courses in October 1989. Much will depend upon the experience of this first cohort of school leavers, not only how they perform in these first AS examinations, but also how their applications are handled by university and polytechnic admissions officers.

It is quite clear from the discussion that followed Professor Wake's talk that an act of faith is required by both sides, the universities and the schools. Furthermore, it is also quite clear that if AS levels are to spread so that by 1990 all schools and colleges are offering some choice in them, the universities and the polytechnics must respond immediately and positively to those who possess the new AS qualification. During the current admissions round and the next, admissions officers will need to show, through their actions, that they are not a cautious, conservative group of individuals, as they have been portrayed. At the very least they must accept that the average points scored on two AS subjects is equivalent to the same number of points scored on a single A level subject. If they were to go further and assert — through their offer levels — that a given number of points scored at AS level is preferable to the same number of points scored at A level, this would not only be realistic but would also convey the right signal to the schools and the students, encouraging them to think of two AS subjects as a desirable alternative to the third A level. The schools, or rather the sixth formers choosing the courses, would then surely respond positively.

While this sort of response from universities and polytechnics is vital if sixth formers are to develop confidence in the value of AS levels, unfortunately it is not sufficient. It is also necessary for them to reconsider their specific course requirements. As Clive Wake has commented, the greater the number of specified A levels that are required to enter a particular course in higher education, the fewer are the options that are left open to the individual who tries to meet those specific course requirements. And in the case of someone who is not sure which of two possible degree programmes he wishes to pursue at university, there may be no choice at all but to take three specified A levels. If AS levels are to be encouraged, and the broadening of the curriculum that results from this is to be achieved, then it is necessary to minimize the number of specified A levels.

For many social science and humanities subjects there is no real problem because an A level in the main subject of the degree is not a specified entry requirement. The main problem areas are in the sciences, including mathematics, and in traditional foreign language degree programmes. Where sixth formers are not certain which science degree course they ultimately wish to follow, the need to keep their options open will often dictate that they opt for a three science A level combination. Only when degree courses in science allow them to enter with AS levels in the main and supporting subjects rather than A levels will they be deflected from the risk averse strategy of taking three science A levels.

Although some universities have already revised their specific course requirements they are a minority and there is an urgent need for others to do likewise. There are already unfilled places on many science courses and problems of recruitment into such courses will be exacerbated by the demographic downturn which will continue into the mid 1990s. Substituting AS requirements for A level requirements will widen the recruitment base for science courses. There are two reasons for this. First, for those coming through the traditional route of sixth form studies there are likely to be more applicants with A or AS qualifications in a particular subject than there would have been candidates with only A level in that subject had the AS option not existed. Second, in the case of those coming up through non-traditional routes such as access courses the gap that has to be closed by such courses will not be so great since clearly, in content at least, access courses will need to be equivalent to about half an A level syllabus rather than the whole syllabus. Thus there might be an increase in the supply of mature students applying to enter science access courses and, other things being equal, the more that enter such courses the more that are likely to succeed and proceed into higher education. At the same time, if specified A levels give way to specified AS levels, it is less likely that acccess courses will be perceived to be diluting standards of entry and admissions officers are likely to be more willing to admit students from them. In summary, if the content of access courses is adjusted in line with the content of AS courses there might be more people willing to join access courses, and a greater willingness on the part of admissions officers to accept them.

Universities have revised their general entry requirements to take account of AS levels. It is now in the interests of each institution to take a close look, subject by subject, at its specific course requirements. Collectively, the universities have it within their power to encourage the spread and development of AS levels, or to kill off what has been an encouraging start. But it is not only within their power, it is in their own interests too to see AS levels become more popular. Although they might not be interested in exercising their power, it is to be hoped that — on this occasion at least — they will be motivated by self interest.

List of Contributors

T.M. Axon is the Headmaster of Ridgeway Comprehensive School, Swindon, Wiltshire.

D.L. Blake is the Academic Vice-Principal of South East Essex Sixth-Form College, Essex.

James J. Hughes is Pro Vice-Chancellor and Professor of Industrial Relations at the University of Kent at Canterbury. He has responsibility for policy relating to undergraduate recruitment and admissions.

D.J.E. Ingram is the Vice-Chancellor of the University of Kent at Canterbury. He is Chairman of the editorial board of the CVCP annual publication, *University Entrance: The Official Guide.*

Robert Jackson, MP, is the Parliamentary Under Secretary of State, Department of Education and Science.

M. Kingdon is Head of Research at the University of London School Examinations Board, London, WC1.

Simon Loveday was a Subject Officer for the University of Oxford Delegacy of Local Examinations, Summertown, Oxford. He is now a Management Consultant with Mosaic Management Group Ltd., Bristol.

Paul Scruton was Principal Professional Officer, Secondary Examinations Council, London, W11.

Clive Wake was Secretary to the Standing Conference on University Entrance, London, WC1. He is now Chairman of the School of European and Modern Language Studies at the University of Kent at Canterbury.

P. Watkins was Deputy Chief Executive of the Schools Curriculum Development Committee, London, W11. He is now Deputy Chief Executive of the National Curriculum Council, York.

156

Index